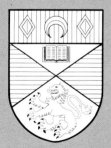

CW00712542

A
WORLD
OF
LEARNING

*University
Collections in
Scotland*

by Laura Drysdale

HMSO EDINBURGH

The Scottish Museums Council is an independent company principally funded by the Secretary of State for Scotland. The Council's purpose is to improve the quality of local museum and gallery provision in Scotland. This it endeavours to do by providing a wide range of advice, services and financial assistance to its membership in the independent and local authority sectors.

Scottish Museums Council
County House
20–22 Torphichen Street
Edinburgh EH3 8JB

A WORLD OF LEARNING

ACKNOWLEDGEMENTS

The work of the Scottish University Collections Research Unit has been funded by the Principals of the Scottish Universities, the Carnegie Trust for the Universities of Scotland, the MacRobert Trusts, the Museums and Galleries Commission and the Scottish Museums Council.

My thanks go to the members of the Management Committee of the Scottish University Collections Research Unit for their advance planning, for their invaluable support in smoothing the path of research within each university, and for their guidance in pursuing the project's aims and objectives:

Professor Frank Willett (Chairman), University of Glasgow;
Charles Hunt, University of Aberdeen;
Dr Hugh Ingram, University of Dundee;
Dr Duncan MacMillan, University of Edinburgh;
Dr Maureen Meikle and Dr Norman Reid, Heriot-Watt University;
Professor Martin Kemp and Dr David Sinclair, University of St Andrews;
Valerie Walker, University of Stirling;
Laura Hamilton, University of Strathclyde;
Tim Ambrose, Director of the Scottish Museums Council.

My assistant, Nuala Lonie, administered the project with great efficiency, and I have been very glad of her help. Finally, I wish to thank all the university curators who gave generously of time and information, enabling us to assemble a full picture of the current state of Scottish university collections, and the Principals of the eight Scottish universities who permitted us to survey their collections.

Laura Drysdale
Project Officer

FOREWORD

The Committee of Vice-Chancellors and Principals of the Universities of the United Kingdom welcomes the publication of this report on the collections held by the Scottish Universities. The existence of many of these collections has hitherto been too little known outside the departments holding them. Now that attention has been drawn to their existence, it is to be hoped that careful consideration will be given, both within and outside the universities, to the collections' future staffing, space and other needs. They constitute an important part of the heritage, not only of each University, but of the nation as a whole.

The report is published as Professor Frank Willett is about to retire from the Directorship of the Hunterian Museum and Art Gallery. It is with pleasure and gratitude that we recognise his contribution not just to this important survey, but to the work and standing of museums and collections generally.

The CVCP acknowledges with thanks the financial support given to the project by the Principals of the Scottish Universities, the Carnegie Trust for the Universities of Scotland, the Museums and Galleries Commission, the MacRobert Trusts and the Scottish Museums Council.

Sir Edward Parkes
Chairman, Committee of Vice-Chancellors and Principals

PREFACE

The Principals of the Scottish Universities were pleased to help fund this important project. It was essential that the nature and extent of the university collections be established and reported on. As a result of the report we are much more aware and appreciative than before of the value and range of the collections entrusted to us. This knowledge will ensure that they are better cared for in future.

Sir Graham Hills
Principal and Vice-Chancellor
University of Strathclyde

PRINCIPAL RECOMMENDATIONS

Direct and effective lines of communication should be established between the University Museums Group as the body representing university collections in Great Britain, and the Universities Funding Council. University Museums in Scotland could offer advice on matters relating to university collections to the Scottish Committee of the Universities Funding Council.

The University Court should recognize that it holds final responsibility for material owned by the university. Each university should establish a Collections Committee, served by a University Curator, which can report to Court on university collections.

A University Curator should be appointed by each university to oversee collections throughout the university. He or she should be appropriately compensated for this work, and should be provided with adequate administrative support. His or her title, responsibility and authority should be recognized throughout the university.

A list of Designated Collections, each with a nominated Curator, should be drawn up by the Collections Committee. These collections should be recognized by the University Court and the Universities Funding Council as having accommodation, staffing and financial needs which must be met. They should at least have access to an identified annual budget, and should be eligible for support from public bodies such as the Scottish Museums Council.

Written collecting policies should be prepared for all Designated Collections, and should be ratified by the Collections Committee and the University Court.

All staff working on Designated Collections, whatever their employment scale, should be eligible for training and travel grants from the university, in order that they may take up available training in curatorship and preventative conservation.

Care of collections should be a priority, with financial provision being made for planned conservation and documentation programmes.

Universities should recognize the value of their collections in promoting the university's image and achievements through prospectuses and other publicity and marketing strategies.

CONTENTS

LIST OF TABLES

The tables comprise information drawn from the collection reports made by the Project Officer after interviewing curators of university collections according to a common pattern (see para 1.19). Because they include information based on assessment, they are intended to indicate the current state of university collections in Scotland, not to give a statistical analysis of the collections themselves.

All 99 collections were used to make up the data, though sometimes information was not available on certain aspects of collections management. This has been noted in the table's title (e.g. *Suitability of space (where recorded)*). Tables drawn from more subjective judgements, for example on the limitations to development in a particular area, have been compiled by recording the number of times certain factors were mentioned. This has also been noted in the table's title (e.g. *Sources of funds (incidents occurring)*).

ABBREVIATIONS USED IN THE TEXT

AMSSEE	Area Museums Service for South Eastern England	OAL	Office of Arts and Libraries
CVCP	Committee of Vice-Chancellors and Principals	RMS	Royal Museum of Scotland
		SCMG	Standing Commission on Museums and Galleries
DES	Department of Education and Science	SDA	Scottish Development Agency
ET	Employment Training	SDD	Scottish Development Department
IT	Information Technology		
MDA	Museum Documentation Association	SED	Scottish Education Department
MGC	Museums and Galleries Commission	SMC	Scottish Museums Council
		STB	Scottish Tourist Board
MTI	Museum Training Institute	SUCRU	Scottish University Collections Research Unit
MSC	Manpower Services Commission		
		THES	Times Higher Education Supplement
NAPIER	National Access to Polymathic Information by Electronic Retrieval	UFC	Universities Funding Council
		UGC	University Grants Committee
NHS	National Health Service	UMG	University Museums Group
NMS	National Museums of Scotland	UMIS	University Museums in Scotland

The former Museum of Natural History at Edinburgh, now the Talbot Rice Art Gallery. From an engraving by W H Lizars used as a heading for letter-paper by Robert Jamieson, Regius Professor of Natural History at Edinburgh and Keeper of the Museum 1804–1854.

1 INTRODUCTION

HISTORY OF UNIVERSITY MUSEUMS

The Connection between Universities and Museums

1.1 The connection between universities and museums stretches back to the origins of both types of institution. From the foundation of St Andrews in 1413 to the present day, Scottish universities have been teaching students, pursuing research and accumulating collections. Though the first public museum in Britain is generally accepted to be the Ashmolean, opened by the University of Oxford in 1683 and based on the contents of the Tradescant Ark and Elias Ashmole's own collection, the presentation of their collections to the University of Edinburgh in 1692 by Sir Andrew Balfour and Sir Robert Sibbald comes a close second. Unfortunately (and ominously in view of the destruction wrought on natural history collections during the 1950s and 60s) this museum, described by Defoe in 1727 as containing a 'vast treasure of curiosities of art and nature, domestic and foreign, from almost all parts of the world' (Murray, 1904), had by 1772 been almost entirely lost.

The Foundation of the Royal Museum of Scotland

1.2 From the foundation of the Sedgwick Museum (Cambridge) in 1727, the Hunterian (Glasgow) in 1807, the Fitzwilliam (Cambridge) in 1816, the Manchester Museum in 1888 and the Anthropological Museum (Aberdeen)[1] in 1907, to more contemporary examples such as the Sainsbury Centre for the Visual Arts (East Anglia) in 1978, the existence of museums pertaining to, but distinct from the academic structure of a university has been well established, and indeed is the origin of the Royal Museum of Scotland.

1.3 In 1812 the natural history collection amassed by the University of Edinburgh since Sibbald and Balfour's gift was given the title Royal Museum of the University and moved to publicly accessible purpose-built rooms in Playfair's new University Quadrangle. In the 1850s, under Professor Jameson's influence, a plan evolved to transfer the collection of some 74,000 specimens to a new National Museum, to be built next door to the university and governed by a separate authority to which the Professor of Natural History would be responsible in his curatorial role. In 1855, the year after Jameson's death, the new foundation was created, comprising a Natural History Museum and an Industrial Museum which in 1864 were amalgamated as the Edinburgh Museum of Science and Art. In 1904 this museum was renamed the Royal Scottish Museum.

1.4 Though initially the university and museum remained closely associated through the shared post of Keeper and Professor of Natural History, and by the physical link of a bridge between the two buildings, relationships between them deteriorated. The museum had agreed that specimens could be borrowed for teaching. Co-ordinating collections became nightmarish, and professors were felt to be neglecting keepership for research. The last straw was the departure of Sir Charles Wyville Thomson on the 1872 Challenger expedition when he had only been Professor for a year. The museum authorities appointed their own Keeper and denied the university access to specimens. A commission was appointed to look into disagreements and the formal connection was severed.

[1] Now known as Marischal Museum.

Informal links do, however, persist with Edinburgh as with the other Scottish universities, all of whom have contributed to the museum's collections (see para 3.14)

Educational Collections

1.5 More hidden, but no less vital to our concerns, has been the growth of collections associated with particular subjects, accumulated either *ad hoc* over many years, or deliberately acquired for research and teaching. Museums have ever been regarded as an educational resource, and within universities were, and indeed in certain subjects still are, essential to teaching and research. Learned societies, such as the St Andrews Literary and Philosophical Society or the Edinburgh Phrenological Society, passed their collections over to the safe-keeping of the university, in the dual interests of preservation and education. David Murray, in *Museums, their history and their use*, published in 1904 at the zenith of specimen-based learning, wrote that:

> Every Professor of a branch of science requires a museum and a laboratory for his department; and accordingly in all our great universities and other teaching institutions we have independent museums of botany, palaeontology, geology, mineralogy, and zoology, of anatomy, physiology, pathology and materia medica, of archaeology—prehistoric and historic, classical and Christian—each subject taught having its own appropriate collection. (Murray, 1904)

The remnants of such enthusiasm are apparent in all four ancient Scottish universities. More recently this concept of a museum's educational value has been applied at Stirling, granted its Royal Charter in 1966. Spurred by the recommendation in the Rosse Report (SCMG, 1963) that the UGC should give equal weight to funding bids for museums as for other university activities, the Department of Biology requested extra finance for constructing a museum area. The request was granted, and a museum opened in 1973. Unfortunately, the UGC's investment is now threatened. Financial cutbacks, space redistribution, and the development of Stirling's Business Studies School have all encroached on the purpose-built area, so that much of the collection is now stored and its teaching value substantially diminished.

Shifts in Taste; the 1960s and Early 1970s

1.6 This cycle of growth and decline, of acquisition and disposal, has recurred throughout the history of university collections. What was vital to one generation has seemed worthless to another. University development in the 1960s led to charters being granted to four Scottish foundations (Dundee, Heriot-Watt, Stirling, Strathclyde) to supplement the four existing ancient universities (Aberdeen, Edinburgh, Glasgow, St Andrews). Over this period the acquisitions/disposal continuum was particularly apparent. While support for traditional material declined, the new universities deliberately created collections illustrating their progressive outlook and their sense of local identity. The pattern was exemplified in Dundee, whose Royal Charter was granted in 1967, transforming Queen's College of the University of St Andrews into the University of Dundee. During construction of the Tower Building in the early 1960s, subsequent to previous dispersal of items from the collection, much of the remaining Queen's College Zoology Museum was discarded, while simultaneously the University bought works of art. We may regret the loss to Dundee of many of D'Arcy Thompson's specimens but can only commend the far-sightedness of a purchasing programme that endowed the University with a fine collection of modern Scottish painting.

Sculpture by Barbara Hepworth at Stirling University.

The Last Ten Years

1.7 It was really from the late 1970s that the funding crisis in universities became acute. No Scottish university has emerged unscathed from the last decade, and all have seen collections suffer from the pressures of competition for diminishing resources within a framework of falling student numbers. St Andrews Archaeological Museum shut in 1988 after the closure of the Archaeology Department in 1986; Strathclyde and Dundee have lost their Geology Departments with collections being transferred to the Hunterian Museum; Heriot-Watt no longer teaches Pharmacy, and the interesting pharmaceutical collections are now in temporary storage under the archivist's charge. These are but selections from a wider spectrum of closure and amalgamation occasioned by the tremendous upheavals of the last ten years, for as departments are costed or funded on bases that inhibit expenditure on non-research, non-teaching activities, so support for collections inevitably declines.

1.8 The most vulnerable collections are those with insecure university status, effectively disenfranchised by association with a dying department and lack of independent access to central administration through a Collections Committee. The Hunterian Museum's practice of nominating identified individuals as honorary Assistant Keepers, responsible to the Director who is himself answerable to a university committee goes beyond tokenism (see para 3.18). By bestowing Hunterian Museum numbers and catalogue entries on items in departmental collections, they are protected by overt university ownership—a wise precaution in a period where Glasgow has seen its grant cut by 20 per cent since 1980, with the loss of 502 posts from 1980–85, and a projected target loss of 300 more from 1985–90.

The Developing Sense of Crisis in University Museums

1.9 The scale of the crisis facing university museums was described at the

Part of the Hunterian Museum's award-winning exhibition on the history of the University of Glasgow, showing a reconstruction of James Watt's workshop. The Museum plays a key role in the University's public relations, with exhibitions, enquiry services, education and research programmes forming a valuable link between the University and the outside world.

1986 Museums Association conference by Alan Warhurst (Warhurst, 1986) and Frank Willett (Willett, 1986), both identifying the potentially disastrous effects of cutbacks in university funding for museums unprotected by any defined funding and management structure. In 1987 a University Museums Group (UMG) was formed, aiming to improve the status and effectiveness of museums, to assist in the identification and listing of university collections and to present a united voice from universities to the University Grants Committee (UGC). The notion that the UMG should act as a UGC advisory panel was accepted in principle by the UGC Chairman in 1987, but has never been formally enacted.

Recent Developments and Future Possibilities

1.10 In his 1986 paper Alan Warhurst saw 'a triple crisis—a crisis of identity and purpose; a crisis of recognition; compounded by a crisis of resources'. The position could only improve from such a low ebb, and indeed as we look to the present, the tide does seem to have turned from an atmosphere of resigned disappointment to one of tentative hope.

1.11 The crisis of identity and purpose, evident for instance in biological science collections where the thrust of teaching now tends to be away from the use of gross specimens and towards bio-chemistry, has had incidents of resolution. Models of good practice, where collections are used in innovative undergraduate teaching and in continuing education and leisure-learning programmes, demonstrate a positive approach to the shift from inward- to outward-looking attitudes manifest in successful universities. Curricular changes in Scottish schools will bring pupils and students further into contact with museums through development of project work, as will continuing education programmes run through university extra-mural departments and distance-learning packages. Prize-winning exhibitions have been mounted in university museums at Aberdeen and Glasgow, and displays appear with less public recognition in departments throughout Scottish universities. The MGC Registration scheme, which is due for adoption in Scotland in 1990–91, will do much to ensure that standards are maintained, and that university curators have increased contact with their colleagues in other museums. Progressive curators and management are recognising that university museums are the institution's valuable public face—a way, in marketing terms, to promote the product.

1.12 This report belongs to the drive to address the crisis of recognition, penetrating the obscurity shrouding university collections by providing concerned organisations with data on their contents and importance. The question of recognition extends, however, beyond the actual objects to their place within the structure of university management, the position of their curators who may be hard-pressed to fulfil formal contractual obligations let alone their informal curatorial responsibilities, and the long-term provision that can be made for the care of collections. The compounding crisis is indeed one of resources. Being peripheral to both university and museum funding agencies and professional bodies, the anomalous position of university collections means that they invariably draw the financial short straw. Protection afforded by Special Factor status, which theoretically ensures that museum funding is maintained in proportion to that for the rest of the university, seems unreliable. Resources of money, space and staff all need to be reviewed if university collections are to play their proper part in public life, upholding professionally acceptable standards of object management and care.

BACKGROUND TO THE REPORT

1.13 Since at least 1963, when the then Standing Commission on Museums and Galleries published its *Survey of Provincial Museums and Galleries* (SCMG 1963), the state of university museums has regularly led to expressions of concern both in specific enquiries and within reports on museum provision generally. Little seems to have changed since the report found that:

> The priority of museums as objects of this (UGC) expenditure is not high, and with the present overwhelming

need, in a period of quite inadequate finance, for increasing the number of undergraduates, the allocation of Government funds to university museums is unlikely to increase for the next few years. Their purchase grants are particularly vulnerable, and, although university museums are in some ways favourably placed for gifts and bequests, we are concerned at the low level and uncertainty of their own resources for this purpose.

Our own review reveals a comparable picture to that existing in 1963. It also makes similar general recommendations, for recognition of the value of museums by the universities themselves, their funding bodies, government departments and local authorities, in a far less propitious economic climate.

Other Reports and Initiatives

1.14 Nevertheless, as we progress through descriptions of university museums in the Wright Report (DES, 1973), the Drew Report (SCMG, 1978), and the Miles Report (MGC, 1986), with specific surveys by the Standing Commission in 1968, 1977 and in its 1986–87 Annual Report, we do appear to have reached a position where words are being transformed into deeds. In 1987, the Museums Association added its voice to these others with a policy statement which outlined areas of concern and called for a comprehensive listing of collections and museums in universities. The 1984 survey of the University of London's collections (Bass, 1984a) has recently been updated in a report calling for coherent action on disparate collections (Arnold-Forster, 1989). Considerable progress in the relationship between the bodies responsible for universities and those working for museums is indicated by joint funding for the Northern England University Collections Survey

from the Committee of Vice-Chancellors and Principals and the Universities Funding Council (UFC) on the one hand, and from the Museums and Galleries Commission (MGC) and the three Area Museum Councils involved on the other.

Involvement of the Scottish Museums Council (SMC)

1.15 Area Museum Councils have helped to raise consciousness about university collections both in universities and in the museum profession (see para 5.17). The SMC's practice of offering members specific collections surveys, supplemented by its series of national collections research projects, has so far produced data on natural science collections (Stace, Pettitt and Waterston, 1987), industrial collections, and the conservation needs of Scottish museums (Ramer, 1989), all of which included university collections. Individual studies on Aberdeen University Museums, the University of St Andrews Archaeological Museum and on aspects of Edinburgh University/Lothian Health Board medical collections, have had a significant impact on the management of those collections, as more generally has the SMC's grant-aid programme, which in 1989 recommended a total (including grants approved in principle) of £88,621.29 to university museums for projects ranging from storage of Aberdeen's reserve collections to support for Edinburgh's presence at the Schools Museums and Galleries Resources Fair. All the Scottish universities are full members of the Council and are therefore eligible for these matching grants; a healthy return on a subscription investment of £419.75 (1988–89). The SMC's support for this university collections project can therefore be seen as embodying two strategic thrusts—firstly in accumulating detailed data on Scottish museum collections; and secondly, in supporting improved collections management with professional guidance and grant-aid.

Scottish University Museums

1.16 Representatives of Scottish university museums came together when Professor Willett, Director of the Hunterian Museum and Art Gallery, convened a meeting in 1985 where the notion of a Scottish university collections research unit was first mooted. The desire to develop communication links and knowledge about collections led to the formation of an informal group, University Museums in Scotland (UMIS) in 1986, which contributed to the MGC Working Party on Museums in Scotland's regard for university museums as an integral part of the Scottish museums community. The report of that working party, *Museums in Scotland* (MGC, 1986), notwithstanding a disappointing response from the Scottish Office, made a number of influential recommendations in its investigation of university museums. It suggested that each university should designate a senior member of staff to chair a university museums committee and take an overview of all university collections; that academic members of staff responsible for collections should be correspondingly relieved of academic duties; that UMIS should continue to meet; and that there should be increased input from local authorities. Whilst funds were being raised for the present survey of Scottish university collections, the MGC asked all Area Museum Councils to commission regional surveys recording the size, scope and purpose of each university collection; how it was being used; what plans there were for its development; who was responsible for it; and how it fitted into the university structure (MGC, 1987).

NATURE AND SCOPE OF THIS SURVEY

1.17 The Scottish University Collections Research Unit (SUCRU) was established in 1988 to: improve awareness of collections and provide an objective basis for decision-making both by individual Scottish Universities and by the UGC (UFC); to identify and locate collections held by Scottish Universities; to describe their nature and range; to identify the current financial provision for collections; to estimate the importance and approximate size of these collections; to compile lists of major donors to or originators of the collections; to record the use made of them in teaching and research, both within the University and outside; to recommend in general how the care of collections might be improved; and to identify sources of advice and support in improving the management of collections.

1.18 The Unit was set up at the SMC after a fund-raising exercise brought contributions from the Principals of the Scottish Universities, the Carnegie Trust for the Universities of Scotland, the MacRobert Trusts, the MGC, and the SMC itself. A Project Officer and a part-time administrative assistant were appointed, reporting to a Management Committee chaired by the Director of the Hunterian Museum and including representatives of each of the Scottish Universities as well as the Director of the SMC.

1.19 Work was divided into two phases. Phase One consisted of abstracting relevant information from data already held at the SMC and elsewhere, visiting the universities and interviewing curators according to a standard pattern, providing curators with simple data sheets to fill in which focused on particularly interesting material, and finally compiling this information into confidential visit reports for each collection. Phase Two involved editing visit reports,

1.1 Priorities and plans outlined in collection reports

The following information is drawn from the priorities and plans outlined at the end of each collection report. Suggestions by both the curator concerned and the project officer have been compiled to give an idea of areas where the greatest need for development and improvement arise.

Categories have been broken down to indicate the variety of issues covered under a particular heading.

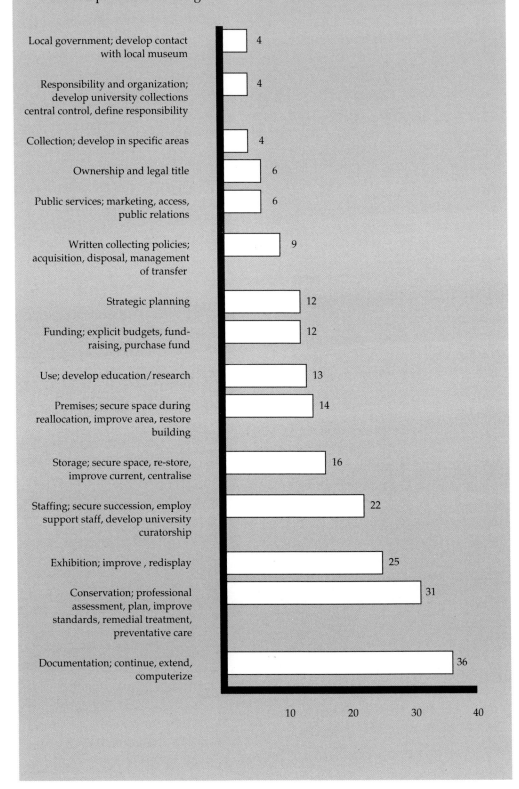

collating the information therein, extending research to look more generally at factors affecting university collections, and writing the final report. Information from the data sheets has been put onto the National Museums of Scotland National Access to Polymathic Information by Electronic Retrieval (NAPIER) system where it will be accessible (given the constraints of normal security provision) to museum curators; the Principals of the Scottish Universities have been sent printouts of their own data, and copies of reports on collections within their university. A third post-publication phase is envisaged, whereby the work of documenting the collections begun by this project might continue on a more detailed basis, consistent with the overall plans of the NMS documentation unit to compile a database for all Scottish museum collections.

1.20 This report follows the format of the interview guidelines which were used during the collection visits. We look at the universities and their collections, at the management of collections, their care, and their use. Those wishing to pursue specific enquiries on individual collections should refer either to the SMC or the relevant university curatorial contact listed in the Appendix.

1.21 As the first such unit to be established in a planned survey of university collections throughout Britain, the Scottish survey addresses issues relevant to universities beyond its immediate geographical boundaries. Scottish universities are not funded independently, though the Scottish education system is markedly different from the English in several respects, and Scottish museums come under the remit of the Scottish Education Department (SED), not as in England the Office of Arts and Libraries (OAL). Our purpose throughout the project has been to address the issues realistically rather than idealistically, placing university collections not only in the comparatively unfamiliar context of the wider museum industry, but also in that of the pressures currently weighing on British universities. The report draws attention to the positive role of collections in university life, though we have also addressed the problems of controlled disposal and transfer which are ever present in institutions whose primary task is the pursuit of learning, with the accumulation of collections being a secondary effect. Our aim is therefore not to suggest unworkable solutions but rather to examine ways for universities to take maximum advantage of their considerable cultural assets.

Astronomical instruments bequeathed to the University of Glasgow in 1754 by Alexander MacFarlane, a former student; part of the Hunterian Museum Historical Collection.

TYPES OF MUSEUMS AND COLLECTIONS

2.1 We have identified 99 collections among Scotland's eight universities, a far greater number than had previously been supposed, indicating that the 46 British universities must contain correspondingly more collections than hitherto identified. The closest estimate to date of the extent of university collections was made by the MGC in its 1986–87 report, referring to over 150 collections in the 46 UK universities, of which 76 hold 'material which as a whole would cause concern at national level if it was under threat of loss, sale or export' (MGC, 1987).

2.2 The UFC admits just 16 museums in 11 universities to its list of Non-Departmental Special Factors with another six museums in six universities as Departmental Special Factors. Special Factor funding is not earmarked but included in an amount passed over to the relevant universities calculated to a complex formula (see para 5.3). Just how little information has been assembled about university museums is demonstrated by

some further references. The Miles Report identified 'at least 37 ... collections in Scotland, of which 18 are open to the public on a regular (although not necessarily on a frequent) basis' (MGC, 1986). In the *Manual of Curatorship* Warhurst noted 50 museums attached to British universities, 'many of which are little more than aggregations of specimens which are, or have been useful to the research and teaching functions of a university department' (Warhurst, 1984). A report published by the Bow Group in 1988 seemed to pluck a figure of 21 university museums from the ether (Goodhart, 1988).

What is a University Museum?

2.3 As Warhurst recognised in his 1986 Museums Journal article, the standard definition does not hold. 'An institution which collects, documents, preserves, exhibits and interprets material evidence and associated information for the public benefit' (Museums Association, 1986) is not applicable to a herbarium though it is indisputably a university collection.

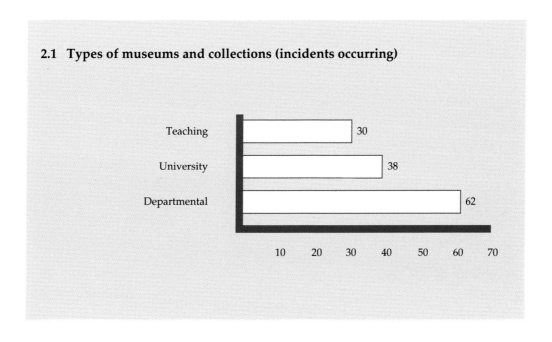

2.1 Types of museums and collections (incidents occurring)

Teaching	30
University	38
Departmental	62

Nor is it enough to say, as Warhurst acknowledges, that 'A university museum is a museum whose building is owned by a university; whose collections are owned by a university; and whose staff are employed by a university' (Warhurst, 1986). This would exclude the eight collections we surveyed sited in premises owned by the National Health Service. As he goes on to suggest, 'What we are really talking about is university collections, some of which happen to be in museums' (Warhurst, 1986).

2.4 At its inception, the Scottish University Collections Research Unit (SUCRU) Management Committee identified three levels of collections:

1) Collections in established university museums.
2) Departmental collections—normally assembled for teaching purposes, but which may no longer have a teaching function.
3) University collections, e.g. paintings, furniture, silver etc not assembled for teaching purposes.

Established university museums are comparatively secure members of the broader museum community, unlike either departmental collections or university collections. These have been taken to include not only the materials itemised by SUCRU, but also groups of objects which are not departmentally specific, for instance scientific instruments at Strathclyde falling within the remit of the Curator of the Collins Gallery. Departmental collections can be simultaneously denoted teaching collections, since they may still be in use. However, many have become redundant for teaching, or contain material which has accrued to a department for various reasons, but commonly through the interest of a particular member of staff. They are the prevalent type of collection, occurring in 62 instances.

Groups of Materials Covered by This Survey

2.5 Six broad groupings of material type have been made, though naturally these are capable of almost infinite subdivision: archaeology and anthropology; natural science; medical science; scientific instruments and apparatus; fine and decorative art; artefacts within archives and libraries. Typically, university support for collections has been concentrated on the fine and decorative arts, focusing on silver, furniture and paintings which have usually been the responsibility of the university secretariat. This bias has been evident in the representation of university collections and therefore in their funding, despite the evidence that natural science and scientific instrument collections are the two types of material most often found in university collections. Only two of the 16 Non-Departmental Special Factor museums hold scientific collections (the Hunterian Museum and the Manchester Museum), and though the Chairman of the UGC acknowledged this bias at a UMG meeting in April 1988, nothing has been done to redress it. Scottish University Principals, whatever their own academic background, have generally been more interested in collecting works of art (for example at Dundee, Stirling and Heriot-Watt) than in protecting other materials; the Principal's support for Edinburgh's newly reopened Zoology Museum is a welcome exception.

2.6 Art collections (silver, furniture, decorative and fine art) have of course the virtue of value, with a market price which can seldom be equalled by other objects. Other collections are given status primarily according to their usefulness, and are therefore at risk if they fall into disuse, especially since they tend to be departmental and may be in-

2.2 Types of material (incidents occurring)

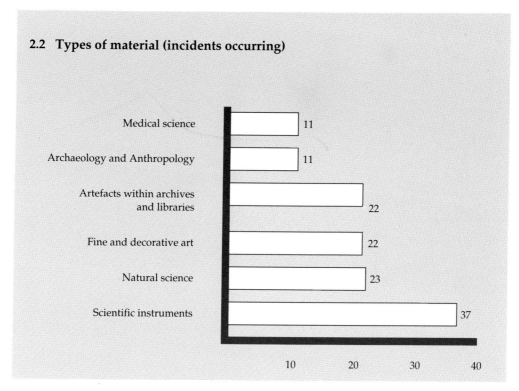

adequately represented at university committee level. Thus though universities may have comparatively well managed central holdings of fine and decorative arts, at the very least listed for an insurance valuation, the bulk of their collections lie scattered throughout various departments, haphazardly catalogued and curated.

2.7 The use of the term *collection* may seem to imply some directed purpose in the original gathering of material, rather than the more usual process of accumulation. The danger of such a distinction is that accumulations can become important in themselves; in Glasgow they form the Hunterian Museum's Historical Collection, which includes the model Newcomen Engine worked on by James Watt, and formed the basis for an award winning exhibition on the history of the university. A definition excluding such material would make it open to disposal.

SOURCES OF MATERIAL

2.8 University collections have similar origins to those in other museums, that is they are acquired by purchase, gift, bequest, fieldwork and exchange, or are on loan. Purchase and donation are the commonest sources of material, occurring in 72 and 74 instances respectively. We found 49 examples of passive acquisition of museum material, for example by accumulation, and 30 cases where material was being actively acquired. There were 22 collections in which no acquisition was taking place.

Purchase

2.9 Purchase may have been purposefully directed, as at Strathclyde where the Collins Gallery has built up an important collection of contemporary Scottish painting over the past five years, or items may have been acquired in the normal course of equipping a department. In the rare cases where allocated purchase budgets for collections do exist, the amounts are pitifully small. As the University Court has resolved that UFC funds may not be used for purchase, the Hunterian Museum employs its income

2.3 Sources of material (incidents occurring)

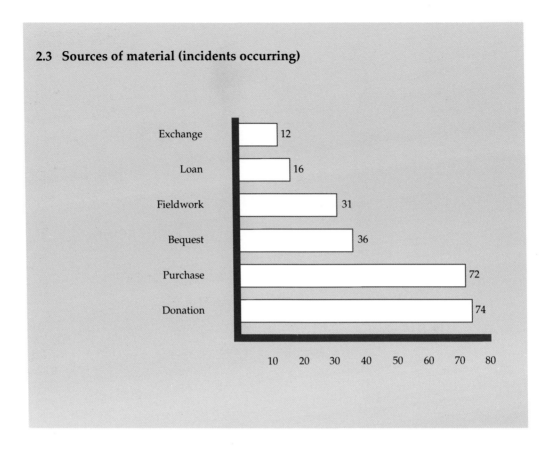

and endowment funds. In the financial year 1988–89, the departments of archaeology and anthropology, coins, rocks and minerals, and fossils each had a £750 purchase budget, amounting to a grand total of £3,000. To put this in perspective, it is worth noting that the Hunterian has a more extensive geology collection than the NMS, houses a coin cabinet of international stature, shares with the NMS the major archaeological collections in Scotland, and holds internationally important first contact 18th century ethnography from Captain Cook's last Pacific exploration. The Hunterian Art Gallery fares rather better because it was able to sell duplicate prints to establish a larger endowment fund in 1982, but even so £14,663 (1988–89) to spend on works of art (excluding prints, for which there is a designated bequest), hardly reflects its international status. Neither the inherent significance nor the local cultural impact of these collections is mirrored in their purchase budgets, which can be compared with an average

acquisition fund of £125,000 in national museums sampled in a recent survey on the cost of collecting (Lord, Dexter Lord and Nicks, 1989).

Donation and Bequest

2.10 Collections have often been passed to universities by donation or bequest because these were regarded both as a safe haven and as a useful scholarly repository. To some extent this may have been due to the misapprehension that universities are public bodies with a concomitant obligation to retain cultural and scientific material for the public good, whereas in fact they are private bodies which paradoxically hold collections in public trust (see para 3.6). Stirling owes its impressive collection of paintings by J. D. Fergusson to his widow, who wished to endow a new, Scottish university and to ensure that the pictures were seen by successive generations of students. During the 1950s many local

26

Voiles Indiennes *by J D Fergusson. One of the collection of paintings given to the University of Stirling by Margaret Morris Fergusson after her husband's death.*

authority museums were divesting themselves of exotic material, retaining only locally significant collections, so that they seemed less secure than universities which were, particularly during the 1960s and early 1970s, in an expansive public-spirited phase.

2.11 Bequests may have conditions which dictate their management. The Curator of the Herbarium at Dundee had to retrieve material from St Andrews when he found it had been transferred there in contravention of bequests, while the Hunterian Art Gallery faced a public

outcry leading to a successful public appeal when it attempted to avail itself of the conditions of Miss Birnie Philip's great Whistler bequest in order to pay for a new purpose-built environmentally controlled art gallery:

I expressly hereby direct that the said University Court shall pay special regard to the desirability of not disposing of the said objects and property in large quantities by a single sale or at one time but shall have the fullest power in its absolute discretion to retain all or any of the said objects unsold for as long as it may think fit and generally to realise them piece-meal or otherwise to the greatest possible advantage in any manner that it may think fit.

Fieldwork and Exchange

2.12 Two additional methods of acquisition which are particularly evident in research collections are fieldwork and exchange. Fieldwork in the natural sciences and in archaeology and anthropology is fundamental to study and inevitably generates a considerable quantity of material. This carries with it the ongoing requirement for storage, conservation, documentation, finance and curatorial time. Clearly such material is at risk of accelerated decay where there is no curatorial presence within a university to monitor conditions.

> The quantitative growth of the world's [collections] has overwhelmed us and become an end in itself, such that we spend all of our time packing away specimens for a research day that never comes. At the same time we find ourselves incapable of retrieving the most elementary information (Shelter, 1969).

Exchange is part of the scholarly process that affects certain subjects such as geology, but it is rarely a source of much material.

SIZE AND GROWTH RATE

2.13 There is no typical size for a university collection. Some collections contain fewer than a dozen items, others more than two million. Disparate as they are in so many respects, the only possible comparisons that can be drawn are within certain subjects. Thus in Edinburgh geology collections amount to some 100,000 specimens, and in St Andrews to around 63,000. A report com-missioned by the OAL on *The Cost of Collecting* (Lord, Dexter Lord and Nicks, 1989) found an overall growth rate of only 1.5 per cent per annum (compared to 4–5 per cent economic growth) in 61 museums which responded to a questionnaire distributed to a selected sample of UK museums, a rate which the authors rightly describe as measured and responsible.

Co-operation and Control

2.14 Because of inconsistent curatorship and documentation, it was difficult to make an estimate of size or growth rate in all but the most controlled situations. Where growth has been recorded, the annual fluctuations which are inevitable when collections depend more on donation and bequest than purchase, illustrate their autonomy both within the university and in the wider context of relations with local and national museums. The situation is improving; instances of co-operation with local authority museums now appear in all the Scottish universities, but no formally agreed collecting boundaries have resulted. The SMC has formed a curatorial panel to examine the Miles Report's (MGC, 1986) recommendation of a semi-formal system of regional natural history reserve collection centres, which would involve university collections in pooling resources with local museums to inhibit duplication.

2.15 Within universities themselves, collections committees (which now meet in six of the eight universities), can monitor acquisition and disposal. The Hunterian Museum's *Sub-Committee on Scientific Artefacts* is empowered to recommend retention of redundant equipment for the Hunterian, donation to the NMS or another museum, and even sale where an item is considered devoid of collection interest, thereby controlling haphazard growth.

External Factors

2.16 Growth may be outside local control, as is the case with the UGC/UFC Earth Sciences Review (Oxburgh, 1987). Five universities with type collections of national importance (Cambridge, Glasgow, Oxford, Manchester, Birmingham) have been designated *Collection Centres*. For Glasgow (i.e. the Hunterian Museum) this entailed instant deposit of approximately 75,000 specimens from Strathclyde and Dundee, and an ongoing commitment to 'act as a repository for future acquisitions from thesis collections, newly published types and figured and cited material, etc.'[1] for all Scottish universities. The museum has to manage a ten per cent enlargement of its geology collection, with an uncertain long-term growth rate. In addition the Department of Geology is expanding; technical staff numbers alone are expected to jump immediately from 12 to 20. More research students generate more research material which needs more curatorial management. In Edinburgh, research posts have doubled from 15 to 30 since 1985, though no provision has been made for matching curatorial facilities to the growth of departmental and research collections which has been stimulated by UGC/UFC policies.

IMPORTANCE OF COLLECTIONS

2.17 The Miles Report's contention that 'the quality of material in Scottish university collections is very high compared with that in most museums in Scotland outside the national collections' (MGC, 1989) is certainly true as far as the Hunterian Museum is concerned; its collections are essentially internationally based, and their formation pre-dates the establishment of Scotland's national museums. However the thesis that *all* universities (and by extension their museums and collections) being funded on a UK basis have a primarily national identity, that staff carry out research work comparable to that in national not local museums, and that collections reflect this lack of parochialism, cannot always be sustained in the face of collec-

2.4   Levels of importance (incidents occurring)

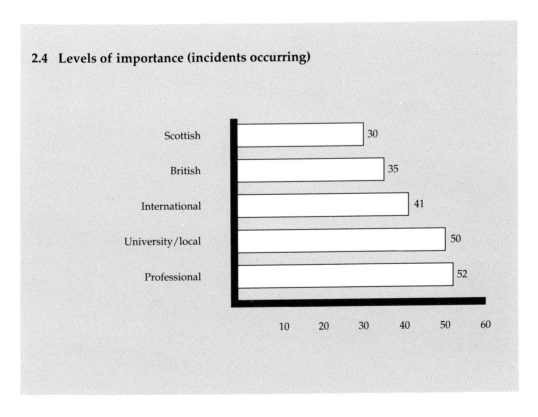

29

tions which are of little significance beyond the boundary of their individual university or department. Forty-one collections are cited as containing items of international importance, and 35 hold items of British importance, though these may be individual pieces or series within a collection of less significant material. The majority hold material which is important either locally, in other words to the university itself, or professionally. This accords with evidence that 53 collections are used in university teaching. Indeed collections of international or national importance may well be of less day-to-day value to a university.

Importance Residing in Function and/or Intrinsic Value

2.18 Gauging importance is difficult because collections often have a dual purpose; a teaching collection may be composed of essentially insignificant material which is nevertheless vital to the educational process. We have distinguished between collections whose status depends on their function (i.e. teaching/research collections which have a professional importance) and those whose importance rests in their intrinsic historic or artistic value. There are some which fall into both camps. For example the Russell Collection of Early Keyboard Instruments in Edinburgh is well used for teaching and research both within the university and beyond, and contains instruments which are inherently valuable.

2.19 Recognition given to a university's past achievements by academic staff and university management affects the importance they accord to collections. However such recognition may have the side effect of identifying objects as saleable commodities, particularly if they are not displayed. The University of Edinburgh has been compelled to consider selling rare books because of a shortage of funds. Sometimes universities seem reluctant to emphasise past achievements in case they obscure the dynamic research image which reaps financial rewards.

Assessing Importance

2.20 Assessment of importance also carries with it the taint of subjectivity. To some extent this can be overridden even in Fine Art where curators can make a knowledgeable estimate of comparative significance. Objectivity has a real basis in the natural sciences, with type and figured material. Assessments made during this survey have been drawn from discussions between the Curator concerned and the Project Officer, and from data held at the SMC. The NMS NAPIER project, which is designed to coordinate documentation in Scottish museums, will at least provide the foundation for a mechanism to gauge the importance of items against each other. Scottish university collections would benefit from comparative assessment by developing an association with the project (see para 6.20).

SUMMARY

2.21 Though scientific instruments are the most common material in university collections, fine and decorative arts have generally been better resourced. Most items in university collections have been acquired by accumulation rather than by directed collecting, but this does not vitiate their contemporary importance, since it has preserved material which otherwise would have been lost. Perhaps owing to this, few collections are composed wholly of material which can be described as important either nationally or internationally, but many contain individual items or groups of material which are of considerable significance.

2.22 Lack of management has produced collections whose size, growth rate, and importance are difficult to assess. Confirmation of the role of a University Curator and a University Collections Committee would help to establish effective methods of monitoring collections as they develop.

Pair of huia birds, formerly found in New Zealand, now extinct. Their remarkably dimorphic beaks enabled the two sexes to perform collaborative and complementary ecological roles. The specimens form part of a display used in undergraduate teaching at Dundee.

COLLECTING POLICIES

3.1 The dearth of written collecting policies, a simple statement of areas of interest and collecting practice, has been deplored in previous reports on university museums. A written collecting policy suggests standards of legal and moral long-term responsibility which any funding body or potential benefactor will expect to see. It ensures that acquisition is kept within reasonable limits, that disposal is responsibly managed, that collections do not needlessly duplicate those in nearby museums, that the University Court is fully apprised of its curatorial obligations, and that legal title is known. Without such a policy it is difficult for universities to discriminate between relevant material and that which merely swells collections to no directed purpose. *Ad hoc* acquisition and consequent lack of a highly developed collection in specific areas reduces the chances of attracting researchers. Confusion can mount so that in crisis, perhaps when there is a possibility of dispersal or disposal, insufficient evidence exists of a collection's rightful status. The position is aggravated where there is no designated curator or committee responsible for collections and no planned care and management programme. Uncertain ownership, often the result of inadequate documentation, leaves collections further unprotected, both locally, and (it seems likely) nationally.

3.2 The MGC Registration scheme, when it comes into operation in Scotland (1990–91), will require written collecting policies and identification of legal title to material. To date only collections in Glasgow and Aberdeen's Anthropological Museum have policies which

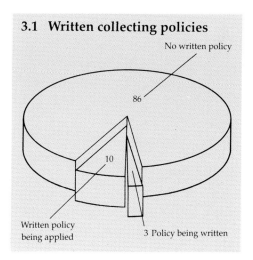

3.1 Written collecting policies

No written policy

86

10

Written policy being applied

3 Policy being written

have been ratified by Court and would therefore meet the scheme's requirements. Such policies are most effectively imposed within the framework of an agreed development plan. The SMC is providing financial and advisory support for drawing up such plans, which it has asked all members to have in place by the end of the Registration process in Scotland if they are to be eligible for grant-aid.

OWNERSHIP AND LEGAL TITLE

3.3 Ownership issues are at the heart of good curatorial practice. Arnold-Forster has pointed out that:

> Clarification of this issue is a fundamental prerequisite of any attempt to secure the future of the collections ... or to seek formal recognition by museum and gallery funding bodies such as the Museums and Galleries Commission or the Area Museum Service (Arnold-Forster, 1989).

Where neither curatorial nor committee representation exists, and where no written policy has been followed, legal title may well be uncertain—a situation which occurs in ten instances in Scottish university collections. The problems are compounded where there is a lack of corporate identity, leaving collections vulnerable to neglect and disposal.

3.4 At St Andrews, radical changes in the functions of the University Court opened a structural gap between collections and university management now filled by an *Advisory Committee on Collections and Exhibitions*. As late as the 1960s Court proceedings found room for what now seem extraordinary points of detail. Changes in location and ownership, and the reports of Committees concerned with objects still appeared as appendices to the minutes of Court meetings in the early and mid 1970s. By the late 1970s they were merely 'on file' via the minutes of the Estates and Buildings Committee; by 1981 they had largely disappeared from Court records.

3.5 The history of the Literary and Philosophical Society of St Andrews collection illustrates the dangers of this gradual diminution of contact between university collections and the Court. In 1904 the University Court assumed responsibility for this collection, which was started around 1840. The ethnographical material, first catalogued in 1884 as holding 146 items (of which few survive in the present collection) included amongst a hotch-potch of curiosities, significant specimens from Australia, Polynesia, Africa and elsewhere. Crucially, since the society was wound up without legal heir, the 1904 agreement between that body and the university ceased to have any legal weight, leaving the collection defenceless against attrition. Repeated moves, at least three fires, dispersal, destruction, donation to other bodies (including the Cupar town collection, the Royal Museum of Scotland and the Rhodes–Livingstone collection in Zambia), and finally closure of the Archaeological Museum, left a member of the Social Anthropology Department with some 68 items to catalogue in 1988. As the curator

suggests in a prescient warning against injudicious disposal, this saga:

> is not only a rather sad reflection on the University Court's solemn pledge to keep the collection in perpetuity but also a reminder of the changing values which have been attributed to non-Western artefacts at different times in the present century (Fardon, 1988).

The University Court as Legal Owner of Collections

3.6 Whilst university museums and galleries differ from local authority and national museums in that they are not technically public bodies, they are commonly perceived to be, and are certainly in receipt of public money. It is likely that donors have regarded them as secure places for their collections in the same way as a publicly owned museum where collections are held in trust and may not be disposed of without recourse to law. There would appear therefore to be an implicit trust that gifts and bequests to university collections are not to be disposed of, unless the terms of the benefaction expressly permit it.

3.7 In most cases (95 in our survey) the University is the acknowledged owner of museum material. We also found 10 examples of privately owned material, and 16 of material which was on loan. The legal owner of any item, even when it has been given or bequeathed to a department, is the University Court (this includes collections made by students acting as members of the university during the course of their studies). However ill-equipped university courts are to discharge the function of trustees, a way must be found of acknowledging the implicit trust placed in them by their benefactors, and of persuading them to accept their public role in this regard despite the private status of universities.

34

Disputed Ownership

3.8 The tradition of departmental autonomy may give rise to dispute, for example where an item has been given specifically to a department. If an element of sharing exists, as in medical departments where members of staff may be paid partly by the local Health Board and partly by the university, and where objects may have been purchased by either partner, a complex situation can arise. At Dundee Dental Hospital, recent threat of closure focused attention on a collection of works of art given to its parent body, a privately owned pre-NHS foundation quite distinct from the present hospital, known as the Institution. The Institution is now subsumed within Dundee Dental Hospital and School, jointly run by Tayside Health Board and the University of Dundee. In the event of closure, who would therefore be the rightful beneficiary of the collection? Ownership remains unresolved.

Transferring Collections

3.9 A further complexity, and one which does not appear to have been addressed by the UGC Earth Sciences Review (Oxburgh, 1987), arises from the process of transfer. Are universities who cede their collection to the local Collection Centre to be compensated? In view of the hawkish attitude manifest towards Glasgow's assets by the Department of Education and Science (DES), it seems surprising that the UGC paid no attention to this issue, and that none of the universities appear to have raised it:

> We are told that there is a substantial collection of pictures and artefacts not included in the financial statements. Although we understand that these are worth many millions of pounds it is unclear to us whether in practice they could be sold to finance deficits, as the collections arise from bequests

or involve constructive trusts (DES, 1986).

DISPOSAL

3.10 Minds are concentrated on legal title when the thorny problem of disposal arises. The Museums Association definition of a museum (Museums Association, 1986) is, as we have seen (see para 2.3), not applicable to all university collections, but it nevertheless provides an ethical framework. In the following paragraphs, the SMC's requirement for full membership has been used, namely the possession of a collection, thus excluding exhibition galleries. Nor have living collections been considered. We are concerned with specimens which do not reproduce themselves and which therefore cannot be replaced in the strictest sense.

Available Guidelines on Disposal

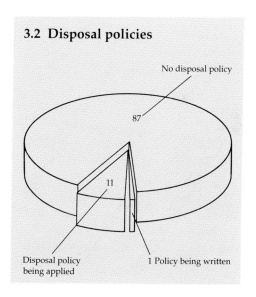

3.2 Disposal policies

No disposal policy

87

11

Disposal policy being applied

1 Policy being written

3.11 It follows from the definition of a museum that a key function is the acquisition of objects to preserve for posterity. The MGC's *Guidelines for a Registration Scheme for Museums in the United Kingdom* (MGC, 1988), which draw on the Museums Association's *Code of Practice for Museum Authorities* (Museums Association, 1986), are a guide to current thinking on the ethics and practice of acquisition and disposal as Registration is intended to encourage museums to attain minimum standards of performance. The paragraphs referring to disposal run as follows:

f)   By definition a museum should have a long-term purpose and possess (or intend to acquire) substantial permanent collections in relation to its stated objectives. Each museum authority must accept the principle that there is a strong presumption against the disposal of any items in the museum's collections except as set out below.

g)   In those cases where a museum is free to dispose of an item (e.g. by virtue of an Act of Parliament or of permission from the High Court or the Charity Commissioners),[2] it should be agreed that any decision to sell or dispose of material from the collections should be taken only after due consideration by the museum's governing body, and such material should be offered first, by loan, exchange, gift or sale to registered museums before sale to other interested individuals or organisations is considered.

h)   In cases in which an arrangement for the exchange, gift or private treaty sale of material is not being made with an individual museum, the museum community at large must be advised of the intention to dispose of material. This should normally be through an announcement in the Museums Association's *Museums Journal*. The announcement should indicate the number of specimens involved, the prime objects concerned and the basis on which the material would be transferred to another institution. A period of at least two months must be allowed for an interest in acquiring the material to be expressed.

i)   A decision to dispose of a specimen or work of art, whether by exchange, sale, gift or destruction (in the case of an item too badly damaged or deteriorated to be of any use for the purposes of the collections), should be the responsibility of the governing body of the museum acting on the advice of professional curatorial staff, and not of the curator of the collection concerned acting alone. Full records should be kept of all such decisions and the specimens involved and proper arrangements made for the preservation and/or transfer, as appropriate, of the documentation relating to the object concerned, including photographic records where practicable.

j)   Any monies received by a governing body from the disposal of specimens or works of art should be applied for the benefit of the museum collections. This should normally mean the purchase of exhibits for the collections but in exceptional cases improvements relating to the care of collections may be justifiable. Advice on these cases may be sought from the MGC.

The Risks of Disposal

3.12 Before reaching a decision to dispose of material it is important to consider that for study purposes, whether of natural objects or of artefacts, ranges of examples are needed. Outside the scope of mass production, scarcely any real duplicates exist. Despite the importance to systematics of the type specimen, it is a variable population that the biologist studies. Change and development in teaching and research may make particular collections redundant at present, but instances where, for example, DNA sequences have been extracted from anatomical specimens, illustrate the danger of jettisoning unfashionable material (see para 7.2).

3.13 The distinction drawn by some museums between de-accessioning (a curatorial decision), and disposal (an administrative function) is academic for

Systematic displays in the Zoology Department at the University of Edinburgh await redisplay and conservation after many years of neglect. Part of the collection has recently been reopened thanks to the efforts of two lecturers supervising an MSC team. The University and the Scottish Museums Council have jointly funded a conservator to work on the collections for a year.

the majority of university collections since so few operate a satisfactory accessioning system. Thirty-four collections in Scottish universities have suffered some disposal, to the regret of their curators. It is fair to say that:

> through lack of adequate initial documentation, numbering and cataloguing, or through subsequent neglect, some of the most famous Scottish natural science collections have been lost or rendered unrecognisable (Stace, Pettitt and Waterston, 1987).

3.14 The vicissitudes of the University of Edinburgh's natural history collections are a salutary reminder that disposal has ever been part of the activity of collecting. The process of discarding specimens to suit different Professors' requirements happened in 1779 under John Walker and in 1804 under Robert Jameson. By 1854 the collections contained some 74,000 specimens which were lost to the University when they were formally transferred to the Royal Scottish Museum after 1872 (see paras 1.3, 1.4). The present material mostly dates from a move to new premises in 1929, and is that which has survived various further purges. In the 1950s the collection was dispersed and the post of museum curator dispensed with when lack of space dictated the need to use the area as a laboratory. Many larger vertebrate specimens were given away or thrown out. The process of regenerating the collection has now started yet again, on the initiative of two lecturers who supervised an MSC scheme in 1987 which has redisplayed and reawakened interest in the collection. A refurbished Zoology Museum was opened in 1989.

Managing Disposal

3.15 It might be argued that disposals are part of the dynamic of intellectual life, but the need for some control over them is incontrovertible. Careful implementation of an acquisition policy may avoid later disposal by redirecting material before it has been formally accessioned. Glasgow's *Sub-Committee on Scientific Artefacts* looks at scientific instruments as they are decommissioned (i.e. before they become collection objects) and decides on their most suitable destination. That post-accession disposal can be effectively handled is demonstrated by the dismantling of the St Andrews Archaeological Museum in 1987, stimulated by UGC withdrawal from funding the Archaeology Department in 1986. Managed in such a way as to ensure survival of the fundamental integrity of the collection, local archaeological material has been transferred to North East Fife District Council Museums Service, who intend to display it in a new museum in St Andrews, while the remaining international material has gone predominantly to the Royal Museum of Scotland (SMC, 1986a).

3.16 Contact with the museum profession can help to salvage material which otherwise would have been lost. The Fibre Science Department at Strathclyde closed recently leaving a number of looms which have now been given to Dundee Industrial Heritage Trust, an appropriate transfer expedited by the Curator of the Collins Gallery on the suggestion of the Director of the Scottish Museums Council.

RESPONSIBILITY FOR COLLECTIONS

3.17 The need for a clear, declared chain of responsibility for collections (which exists in 70 cases) is manifest both by the positive results when such a system exists and by the conversely negative ones where responsibility is either token or obscure. The optimum pattern was described in the Miles Report:

> Each university should designate a senior member of its staff, who is a member of Senate and preferably also a member of Court, to be responsible for all collections as chairman of a museum committee representing and having an overview of all collections within the university. In the same connection we recommend that for each university collection a member of the academic staff be charged with responsibility for the collection and be relieved of academic duties in proportion to his or her recognised curatorial duties involved (MGC, 1986).

Formal Structures

3.18 Scottish universities offer a range of management models for assessment. The Hunterian Museum has evolved a highly structured system by accrediting staff as Honorary Keepers or Honorary Assistant Keepers of the Hunterian Museum in departments with collections. Both the salaried curatorial staff of the museum and the Honorary Assistant Keepers are responsible to the Museum Director, who reports to a *Museums and Galleries Committee* which consists of the six Honorary Keepers, three members of Court, six members of Senate, the Keeper of the Hunterian Books and Manuscripts (the University Librarian), representatives of the Museum and Art Gallery staff, and a student representative. Honorary Assistant Keepers of collections varying from the Hague Collection of wind instruments in the Department of Music to a collection of diagnostic ultrasound equipment in the Queen Mother's Hospital are located in the structure and can refer to the Hunterian Museum for professional advice and support. Thus curatorial attitudes penetrate far into the university's complex organization, stretching from the administrative core of Court and its committees to outlying institutions managed jointly by the University and the Health Board.

3.19 By contrast, the younger and smaller University of Stirling has no single chain of responsibility for collections, and the Curator of University Paintings works within a more fluid system where responsibility for works of art and collections is shared by the Estates and Buildings Office, the Finance Officer and the University Secretary. The growth of one collection (such as the Howietoun Museum of Fish Farming, now being developed) and the decline of another (the Biological Sciences Museum) cannot therefore be viewed in an overall context since no collections forum exists.

Informal Structures

3.20 Informal structures do not necessarily preclude good collections management. At the University of Dundee a *Collections Ad Hoc Advisory Group* is chaired by a Senior Lecturer. Though the group is not a formally constituted Court or Senate committee, it has awakened interest in the collections throughout the university, bringing to light many previously unknown items, and generating concern for collections affected by space reallocation programmes. Court has now instructed the Buildings Officer to take collections into account when planning departmental moves. The group has also persuaded Court to identify, via departmental heads, named individuals with responsibility for collections. Such a flurry of activity shows how stimulating a focal body can be, even without a statutory role.

3.21 The problem with informal structures is also, paradoxically, that which can make them work well—their

dependence on individual enthusiasm. Nevertheless, a formal structure amounts to little without the support of key members of university staff. The University of Edinburgh has a *Pictures, Galleries and Collections Committee* which reports to Court, but crucially it also has a sympathetic University Secretary who has ensured that collections have not suffered disproportionately during the financial crisis of the last ten years. The Talbot Rice Art Centre and Gallery,[1] which with its temporary exhibition programme and its permanent collection is now an indispensable feature of the city's cultural profile, owes much to his support.

The Impact of Personal Enthusiasm

3.22 At curatorial level, personal interest is highlighted since so few collections have salaried professional staff. Where responsibility is seen as burdensome, limiting research progress or teaching time, a collection is likely to fall into stasis or even deterioration, awaiting transformation by an interested individual. Since universities seldom give credit for work relating to collections, curatorship may seem onerous to a career academic. The success of the Natural History Museum at Aberdeen, where the curator is a Senior Lecturer approaching retirement who spends about 30 per cent of his time on the museum, rests on his enthusiasm for the museum and its communicating, conservation role which he is able to maximise because it does not conflict with his career. On the other hand, personal interest may allow management to avoid the real cost and responsibility of employing professional staff. Edinburgh's Reid Collection of Historic Musical Instruments amply fulfils every criterion of professional curatorship, and yet is run by a dedicated Honorary Curator supported by a team of volunteers. Personal interest is often

[1] Now known as the Talbot Rice Gallery.

From the Reid Collection of Historic Musical Instruments, University of Edinburgh:
Serpent by Haye, London, c 1825; Portable harp by J Egan, Dublin, c 1825; Flute by S Koch, Vienna, c 1820;
Flute by Tebaldo Monzani, London, 1816; Set of bagpipes by Hugh Robertson, Edinburgh, 1793.

responsible for creating a collection; the Kelvin Collection in Glasgow's Department of Physics and Astronomy was drawn together by a Research Technologist who catalogued and restored apparatus relating to Lord Kelvin's work. This was housed in a purpose-built UGC-funded display area in the Department. Unfortunately building alterations mean that this space will be lost in 1989–90 and no alternative has yet been secured.

De facto Responsibility

3.23 Departmental collections may be the *de facto* responsibility of a member of staff on account of his or her specialism. The Senior Lecturer in Dental Surgery at Dundee Dental Hospital was appointed as a dental anatomist with implied responsibility for the Comparative Dental Anatomy Collection and by extension of his curatorial role, the Art

Collection. Fortuitously, many such associations work well. However, without the backup support of a designated University Curator able to mobilise an effective Collections Committee, collections are at risk from the slightest change in personnel, research direction, building alteration and so forth. This is what a system of honorary appointments such as that bestowed by the Hunterian Museum avoids, since not even notional responsibility can then be allowed to slip away unnoticed.

ORGANIZATIONAL CONTEXTS

3.24 It is heartening to be able to report considerable development in the numbers and vigour of museums committees since 1986 (MGC 1986). Then only Aberdeen and Glasgow had active committees. Now 78 collections come under the aegis of a Collections Committee and only 21 still have no such representation. Edinburgh's Pictures and Galleries Committee has had its remit extended to cover all collections; St Andrews has instituted an Advisory Committee on Collections and Exhibitions; and Dundee has its Collections *Ad Hoc* Advisory Group. Strathclyde, Stirling and Heriot–Watt have less explicit collections representation.

Connections with University Offices

3.25 Good relations with the central administrative offices of a university, its finance department or secretariat, its estates and buildings or works department and, where there is such a thing, its information office or public relations department, promote successful curatorship. Whether expressed by personal contact or through university offices, curators must be able to call on central administrative support for collections which are scattered throughout the complex structure of university organization.

3.26 The Finance Department/Secretariat, which has traditionally held responsibility for university possessions, including historical and ceremonial material, may retain considerable involvement in any central curatorial role. This may extend to providing financial support, especially where there has been no implicit or explicit funding from the UFC. One example exists at St Andrews, where the Advisory Committee on Collections and Exhibitions receives a small annual conservation grant from the Finance Committee to cover collections throughout the university.

3.27 Estates and Buildings Departments have often been responsible for material associated with university premises. This office has been the agent for the renovation of Stirling's Airthrey Castle, and at Glasgow is supporting a refurbishment programme at the Hunterian because it is alert to the Museum's value as a public face of the university, one important avenue for developing contact with the local community. The Works Department at Dundee has proved invaluable during the recall of paintings which were previously scattered and are now more coherently displayed and curated.

3.28 Where there is an Information Office or Public Relations Office, for example at Aberdeen and Heriot–Watt, the relationship is invariably mutually beneficial. The archivist at Heriot–Watt provides data and displays for the Public Relations Office, with the *quid pro quo* of a fair amount of exposure for the collections in press releases and exhibitions.

Departmental Context

3.29 An important context for departmental collections is their department or school. Individual 'cost centres', as they are now termed by the UFC, may exercise

Portrait of Dr Robert Wilson in Turkish costume before the ruins of Athens, painted in 1824. Dr Wilson was a graduate of King's College, Aberdeen, who travelled throughout the Orient in the first decades of the 19th century, and left his collection of antiquities and curiosities to form the nucleus of a university museum.

considerable autonomy. Universities grow organically not mechanically, with even the newest of them developing according to the success of particular research departments, or in response to student or external demand. As a result, many departments have a stronger sense of their own history and identity than of their connection with the corporate body of the university.

Medical Collections

3.30 University medical schools seem to have a particularly acute sense of independence, perhaps because they have always worked in cooperation with other organizations, whether private institutions or, as now, local Health Boards. The nature of their collections, for example of anatomy, pathology or forensic science specimens (where access is restricted by the Anatomy Act 1984)[3], means that they sit uneasily with the bulk of university material. The specimens themselves are often housed in purpose-built units adjacent to dissecting rooms, and are still integral to teaching despite increasing use of videos, photographs and plastic models. Several historic collections are currently being refurbished, amongst them Edinburgh's Anatomy Department which is raising funds to conserve and redisplay its phrenology collection, and Glasgow's Anatomy Museum which has recently been redecorated, and where the spirit jars containing Dr William Hunter's historic specimens are being refilled by a retired mortuary technician employed on an hourly basis. Medical collections do belong within the spectrum of university holdings and can prove sources of interesting and exhibitable material, as the proposed museum at Ninewells Hospital in Dundee will no doubt demonstrate.

Links to Industry and Commerce

3.31 Historic links to industry and commerce, characteristic of Heriot–Watt and Strathclyde with their background in technical education, can similarly prove more enduring than those with the university itself. The Pharmacy Department at Heriot-Watt, which closed in 1989, held material dating from 1885 when the Watt Institution and School of Arts became Heriot–Watt College. It also contained items from the absorption of the Public Royal Dispensary in 1936, and redundant equipment from local pharmacies. The collection therefore reflects professional development and has aroused the interest of the Royal Pharmaceutical Society who are considering a proposal to open a museum in Edinburgh. It may well be more relevant in its professional context than to the university.

SUMMARY

3.32 It is not surprising, given the shortage of staff and financial resources, that few university collections operate according to written policies on collecting and disposal, though the majority do now have the support of a clear chain of responsibility focused on a University Collections Committee. These links need to be strengthened to ensure that the benefits of individual enthusiasm can be sustained by an established collections structure within each university, and to assist curators in raising collections management to the standards set by bodies such as the MGC and the Museums Association for ethical collecting and disposal.

Innovative redisplay of Aberdeen's Anthropological Museum (now called Marischal Museum) by the Curator and a firm of consultant designers won the Scottish Museum of the Year Award in 1987.

MANAGEMENT OF PERSONNEL AND PREMISES

CURATORIAL STAFF

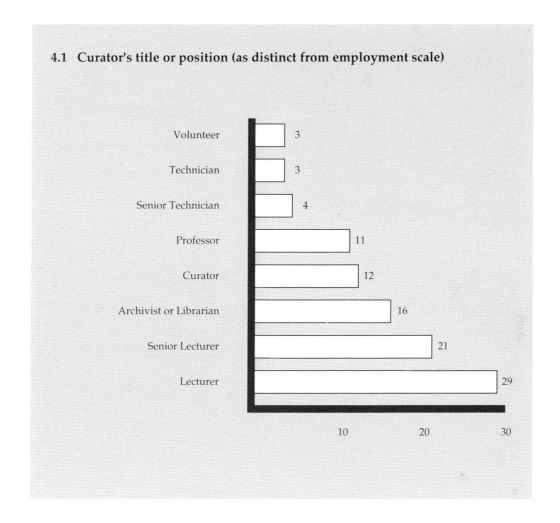

4.1 Curator's title or position (as distinct from employment scale)

4.1 The title *Curator* implies a member of staff employed in a professional capacity in a museum; there are few such in Scottish universities. Most "curators" are academic staff whose main duties lie elsewhere, and continuity of curatorial responsibility is assured in only one third of all cases. The range of levels of curatorship is wide, and can be described in descending order of management commitment.

Curators of University Museums

4.2 Full-time professional curators, employed to run museums recognised as such by the University Court, are in post at the Anthropological Museum in Aber-

deen, the Collins Gallery at Strathclyde, the Hunterian Museum and Art Gallery in Glasgow, and the Cockburn Museum in Edinburgh, which, however, is not publicly accessible to the same degree. Employed staff have an acknowledged position and status; the Curator of the Anthropological Museum is on the same salary scale as the Archivist and the Assistant Buildings Officer, and his voice carries comparable weight. Some curatorial staff at the Hunterian Museum might perhaps be placed in a different category, since they devote a significant proportion of their time (up to ten per cent) to teaching undergraduates. The Senior Curator of Geology, however,

4.2 Curator's background and training

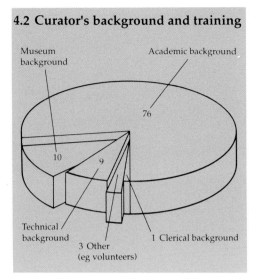

carries 25 per cent of a normal lecturer's teaching load within the Geology Department, and it has often, in practice, been considerably more. Thus the Museum's staff spend a significant amount of time away from their primary curatorial tasks.

4.3 Staff resources may be put in perspective by cross-referencing them to the importance and size of collections. The Hunterian Musem's Geology collection, which is larger (at approximately 825,000 specimens) than the Royal Museum of Scotland's, employs two curators and one technician, compared to the RMS's staff of 12. Should the UFC support the university's bid for three extra staff to cope with the management of 75,000 specimens from Dundee and Strathclyde occasioned by the UGC Earth Sciences Review (Oxburgh, 1987), staffing levels will still be well below par. Edinburgh has several publicly accessible museums: the Cockburn Museum of Geology (some 100,000 specimens); the Reid Collection of Historic Musical Instruments (about 1000 instruments); the Russell Collection of Early Keyboard Instruments (a UFC Departmental Special Factor); and the Talbot Rice Art Centre and Gallery which has a permanent collection of mainly 17th Century paintings and bronzes, and an Art Gallery which mounts between 10 and 12 temporary exhibitions and

organizes between three and six touring exhibitions annually. The sum total of salaried curatorship expended on these collections, all of which contain items of international importance and run exhibition, research and educational activities to a professional standard (albeit with extensive voluntary support), amounts to the equivalent of three full-time posts.

Salaried Curators of Departmental Collections

4.4 Members of staff who have been appointed as Curators within departments may also have other duties. The full-time Geology Curator at St Andrews was appointed in 1981 and now spends an estimated 40 per cent of her time on curatorial duties, with her other tasks being teaching and laboratory work, supervision of fluid inclusion equipment, departmental administration, and participation in outreach educational work. Our data show that though 12 collections are run by staff whose job title is Curator, only nine curators spend 100 per cent of work-time on their collections.

Staff with an Acknowledged Curatorial Role

4.5 Lecturer or technician posts may include an acknowledged curatorial component. Taxonomic botanists are usually expected to curate university herbaria, though there has been a gradual erosion of designated curatorial responsibility in this discipline. Until 1977 Aberdeen's herbarium maintained a full-time Keeper post. This then became part-time and in 1981 was lost as a distinct role. University archivists may act as curators since archives inevitably accrue some artefacts, and at Heriot–Watt this implicit role has become explicit, in that the Archivist there has notional responsibility for university collections. Part-time salaried curatorship may prove exceedingly demanding. The Curator of the Talbot Rice Art Centre and Gallery spends a theoretical 50 per cent of his time teaching in the Department of Fine Art and 50 per cent curating the Art Centre; in reality, he effectively holds down two full-time jobs.

Staff with *de facto* Responsibility for Collections

4.6 Many curators are assumed to be responsible for managing a permanent collection within a department, but are given no time, promotional credit, nor any sort of compensation for curatorship. However to recommend compensation might be dangerous, since it implies a commitment to departmental collections which could conceivably put the collections at risk. A Head of Department might see disposal as a way to maximise available manhours and research input, in which case the university as legal owner ought to take responsibility for the collection.

Pressures on University Staff

4.7 Academics are under pressure on many fronts. UFC rankings are research based, and there is ever higher competition for public and private research grants. Publication plays a vital role in promotion, which in itself is markedly harder to obtain in a climate of frozen posts, new contracts without tenure, and threatened redundancies. Publication unrelated to the main thrust of a department's research interests earns no credit (although conversely, university museum curators may, unlike their colleagues in public museums, be promoted on the strength of their academic work). On the teaching front, expectations are equally demanding, with competition to attract students rising as numbers fall.

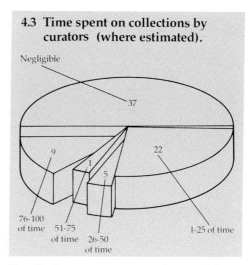

4.3 Time spent on collections by curators (where estimated).

Small departments may be unable to reach the minimum staff/student ratio considered viable by the UFC (20 staff per 200 students), whatever the success of their research programme. Funding crises, management plans and UGC/UFC subject reviews have involved staff in a seemingly endless process of justifying their activities which is time-consuming and can be demoralising.

4.8 Despite the hostile climate, many university collections are well curated on minimal resources, often in the face of mounting adversity. Aberdeen's Natural Philosophy Collection contains some important items dating back to the mid 18th century housed in the Department of Physics, which has been in trouble since 1981. The 1960s building had a suitable museum display and storage area from 1973 to 1985, run by the Honorary Curator (a full-time lecturer) with informal technical back-up. In 1985 the display area was lost to the Department of Engineering, and support was gradually withdrawn from the collection. The instruments were moved to various storage locations though a small display area was retained in the building's foyer. Physics is now merely a service unit for Engineering, but the Honorary Curator has worked with the Curator of the Anthropological Museum to ensure that the collection will be housed in a central university store. As he intended, this implies that the university has accepted its ultimate responsibility for the collection. A historic precedent for tenacious curatorship was set by Professor Butler of the Natural Philosophy Department of St Andrews when he ignored an authorisation by the Court in 1903 to 'destroy such portions of the class apparatus as are useless'. Had he complied, the Historical Scientific Instruments Collection would have lost several items of extraordinary rarity including the great planispheric astrolabe made by Humphrey Cole in 1575 and widely regarded as the finest instrument of the Elizabethan era, and Joseph Knibb's split-second chronometer made in 1677, which is probably the first clock to read to an accuracy of a fraction of a second.

Range of Curatorial Scales

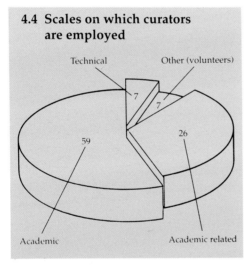

4.4 Scales on which curators are employed

4.9 Full-time professional curators tend to be employed on the Academic Related scales, as do librarians and archivists with a curatorial role. Academic posts are a precious commodity in an era of staff cutbacks and frozen posts, so they may be hijacked from curatorship to teaching and research. For this reason the two assessors of Collection Centres' bids for the ongoing implementation of the UGC Earth Sciences Review have recommended that curatorial posts created to manage the transfer of geological material between universities should be

on the Academic Related scales. Curators with a primarily academic role have limited access to curatorial training and travel grants, since they need to retain travel funds for attending conferences in their subject. The position is no better for Academic Related staff, who are generally ineligible for university travel grants.

4.10 Curators on technical grades may be over-qualified for this level of employment, an all too common feature in museums. The Geology Collection at St Andrews is run by a full-time curator whose doctorate has not influenced her employment on a technical scale. Although the preferred scale for curatorial employment is the Academic Related, it may be better for a collection to be administered by a technician than by a lecturer who is less likely to have any allocated time for curatorial duties. However succession is particularly uncertain for technical grade posts, which have been disproportionately hard hit by staff cutbacks (see para 4.11). Unfortunately technical grade staff who run teaching collections and who could benefit greatly from the sort of in-service training offered by the SMC, are also ineligible for training and travel grants, and are thereby distanced from advice on good curatorial practice.

SUPPORT STAFF

Technical and Secretarial Staff

4.11 Financial constraint has led to a widespread loss of technical posts and support staff. Since 1981, the Anthropological Museum at Aberdeen has lost two technical staff, one attendant and a half-time secretary. Lack of support staff has a knock-on effect on other museum activities. Since his technician was not replaced in 1981, the Curator of Coins and Medals at the Hunterian Museum has added casting reproductions to his other roles as museum security officer,

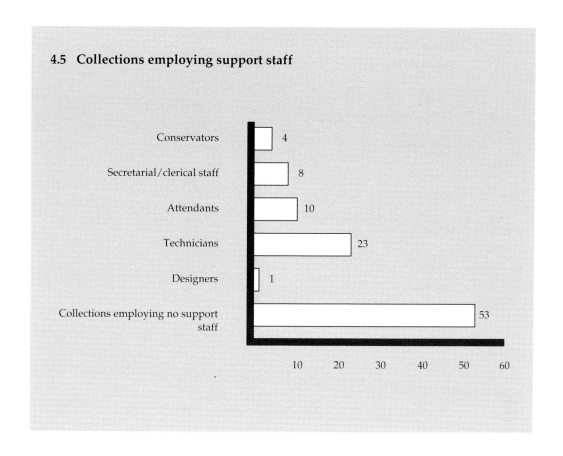

4.5 Collections employing support staff

Conservators 4
Secretarial/clerical staff 8
Attendants 10
Technicians 23
Designers 1
Collections employing no support staff 53

museum temporary exhibition officer, university teacher, and curator of an internationally important coin cabinet.

4.12 Support staff are vital to the proper running of collections, a point frequently lost on those responsible for funding museums in universities and elsewhere. The appointment of a Senior Secretary for the Curator of Edinburgh's Talbot Rice Art Centre and Gallery has released the Curator from the burden of administration so that he can use his expertise to best advantage. The Curator of the Collins Gallery at Strathclyde is hampered in her outreach work, educational initiatives and fund-raising programmes by lack of technical support to instal her annual schedule of ten temporary exhibitions.

Attendants

4.13 Attendant staff are essential for the secure opening and supervision of a museum, and yet they are specifically employed for only ten collections. The Anthropological Museum at Aberdeen has been advised by the SMC and the Scottish Tourist Board (STB) that its disappointing visitor figures (18,000 in 1988 according to the STB's records), could be raised by opening the museum on Saturdays. The museum opens for three hours on Sunday afternoons, and weekend opening generally is under review. Staff shortages, however, may preclude major changes. Edinburgh's Talbot Rice Art Centre and Gallery, which like the Anthropological Museum is on first floor premises with no street frontage, but which has two attendants and is open on Saturdays from 10am to 5pm during exhibitions, had 23,000 more visitors in 1988 (STB, 1988). The MGC's use of a photograph of the Hunterian Museum with a sign saying 'We regret Main Hall closed due to staff shortage' (MGC, 1987) as the cover of its 1986–87 annual report featuring university collections was apt indeed.

OTHER STAFF

Government Employment Training Schemes

4.14 The change from Manpower Services Commission (MSC) schemes to Employment Training (ET) has mostly been unwelcome in museums. The loss of trainee cataloguers, curators, technicians, exhibition designers and constructors, public relations officers and education officers—to name but some of the employment opportunities offered by university museums in Scotland under previous schemes—has hit this short-staffed area very hard. At the Hunterian Museum and Art Gallery, some 300 staff years of work were provided by MSC trainees from 1976 to 1988. Under ET, the Museum had two trainees who each worked 18 hours per week. Job Creation, Community Programme and Youth Opportunity schemes resulted in numerous ventures, the following amongst them: setting up Edinburgh Anatomy Department's *Death Masks and Life Masks of the Famous and Infamous* exhibition in the 1987 Edinburgh Festival; redisplaying Edinburgh's Natural History Collection; cataloguing Strathclyde's scientific instrument collection; cataloguing and storing Dundee's collection of photographs by the Hungarian photographer Michael Peto; staffing a paper conservation workshop in Dundee's Archive Department; producing display boards and information sheets for St Andrews Bell Pettigrew Zoology Museum; cataloguing scientific collections in various Glasgow departments on behalf of the Hunterian Museum; modernising Glasgow's Herbarium and surveying plants in the area; circulating Glasgow's Veterinary Anatomy collection to schools in a travelling laboratory; and many more.

4.15 The picture is radically different under ET, with only five trainees presently being employed throughout the eight universities. Few university collections are able to fulfil the formal training component of the scheme (two-fifths of a 30-hour working week). ET trainees are carrying out useful work in Dundee's archive, but the archivist has found that training takes up a disproportionate amount of time if there are insufficient trainees to justify employing a supervisor. Subcontracting to a Managing Agency has however eliminated administration and supplied some training, and has also helped to weed out unsuitable candidates. Other curators have found that they are unable to select suitable trainees and have abandoned contact with the scheme.

Volunteers

4.16 Volunteers work in 19 collections, though Curators are often hesitant about using them. Honorary Curators might themselves be described as volunteers, since they receive neither financial nor time compensation for their curatorial work. The Senior Curator of Palaeontology and Stratigraphy in the Hunterian Museum has been partially able to compensate for the loss of technical staff with the help of two volunteers who have been working as technicians once or twice a week over eight or nine years. Students have occasionally helped in the Talbot Rice Art Centre and Gallery and the Collins Gallery, and in other collections where their subject is relevant.

Contracts and Consultancies

4.17 Contract work and consultancies occur in only five cases, as few collections have any budget to spend on them and so mostly use in-house resources. One exception has been the redesign of Aberdeen's Anthropological Museum, which has been undertaken by consultant designers. Management consultancy or conservation consultancy and contracts have often been negotiated through the SMC. The STB has supplied marketing consultancy to certain of the more public collections.

TRAINING

Access to Training

4.18 Training is restricted either by competition for funds for attending academic conferences (for Academic staff), or by university prohibition on training and travel grants for Academic Related and Technical staff. Only 16 curators have been able or willing to take up available training opportunities. An identified need for curatorial training in collection care makes this low access level particularly disturbing. The SMC's *A Conservation Survey of Museum Collections in Scotland* notes that:

> A recurrent theme in the site surveys is the need for some form of training for curators and their staff, not only in the part they can safely play in remedial conservation, but even more importantly in the care of collections, and in recognising the stage at which a conservator needs to be called in (Ramer, 1989).

Short Courses and Modular Distance-Learning Packages

4.19 The SMC is now developing short-term educational programmes to meet this need. The Museum Training Institute (MTI), which has been established by the Museums Association and the Office of Arts and Libraries to instigate museum training programmes, is designing both open and distance learning projects and direct training programmes. The flexibility offered by a system of individual selection from a menu of courses will be valuable to cura-

tors who wish to improve their skills, but for whom curatorial work is a subsidiary activity to their predominant career path. The MTI can also create tailor-made courses where there is a guaranteed audience of at least 15, though naturally this is more expensive than pre-packaged training.

4.20 Training is a high priority need as far as improved care and management of university collections is concerned. Training bodies might take account of the particular difficulties and areas of concern affecting curators in universities, and Collections Committees need to make the case for support for curatorial training to university authorities. Travel and training grants should be available to all curators of Designated Collections, whatever grade they are employed on.

SUMMARY AND POTENTIAL DEVELOPMENTS

4.21 Responsibility without power dulls the spirit of any curator, so access to those institutions and individuals who influence the course of university policy is essential to good management of collections. Collections Committees clearly benefit from the involvement of members of Court and Senate, and it is plain that organizations as federal as universities need an identified University Curator, who reports to the Committee and who is duly compensated for his/her collections responsibility. In the past it may have been enough to rely on the goodwill of individuals and their host departments who have effectively given curatorial time to the University. But as demands on academic teaching and research time grow, time to curate material correspondingly decreases; in 57 instances curators see no potential for increased staffing of collections. The result may be a sorry decline in the state of collections, but it also provides room for the role of a University Curator,

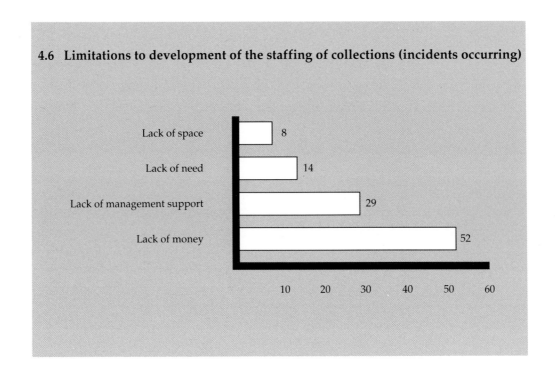

4.6 Limitations to development of the staffing of collections (incidents occurring)

responsible for collections throughout the university.

4.22 There are already moves in this direction outwith the well established system run by the Hunterian Museum and Art Gallery. Since the Miles Report was published (MGC, 1986), the Curator of the Anthropological Museum has been designated Curator of University Pictures (Aberdeen) and the Curator of the Talbot Rice Art Centre and Gallery has become Curator of University Collections (Edinburgh). The Archivist at Heriot–Watt has been given *de facto* responsibility for other university collections, as has the Curator of the Collins Gallery at Strathclyde, and a Curator of University Pictures (with a watching brief over other collections) has been appointed at Stirling. All these Curators are employed in salaried full or part-time posts.

PREMISES

4.23 University collections are housed anywhere from a fully accessible public display space with associated storage areas to a small cupboard in a depart-

mental store. Few premises are wholly structurally unsuitable or in such poor condition as to be causing damage to objects, though many would benefit from improvement. The major source of anxiety regarding premises is insecurity of tenure; many collections have had to move storage and display areas more than once in the last five years, with inevitable disruption and damage to delicate objects and specimens. Alice J. Marshall described moving Glasgow's Pathology Collection in 1967:

> This involved a tremendous amount of work but was accomplished with surprisingly few casualties considering that they had to be man-handled, transferred from shelves to a trolley, transferred again to a trolley and wheeled up an incline to the hut outside (Marshall, 1970).

The Pathology Collection has had to be moved twice since then, into ever-decreasing space. Other collections occupy space on sufferance, perhaps in an area not currently required for another purpose, and so are vulnerable to any change of use.

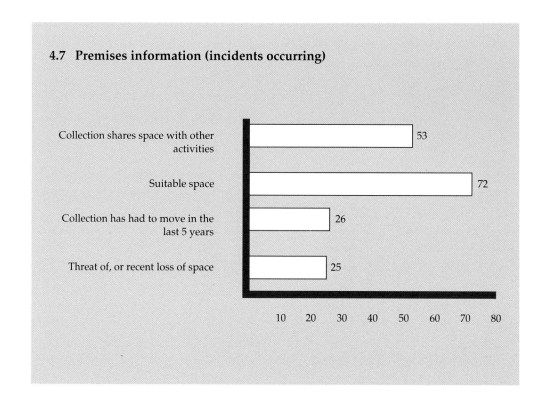

4.7 Premises information (incidents occurring)

Collection shares space with other activities — 53
Suitable space — 72
Collection has had to move in the last 5 years — 26
Threat of, or recent loss of space — 25

Sharing Facilities

4.24 Fifty-three collections share facilities on a permanent basis. This may save overheads, for instance where collections are housed in buildings owned by the National Health Service (NHS). Sharing departmental facilities can however leave collections insufficiently isolated from material in regular use, particularly if stored in lecture preparation rooms, or exposed to the physical risks of display in public circulation areas such as corridors and social spaces.

Space Rationalization

4.25 A common thread in physical disruption to collections is space compression and rationalization resulting from actual or anticipated application of UGC/UFC space norms. In the last five years, 27 collections have experienced

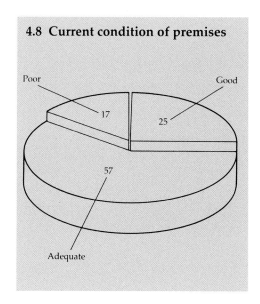

4.8 Current condition of premises

Poor 17
Good 25
Adequate 57

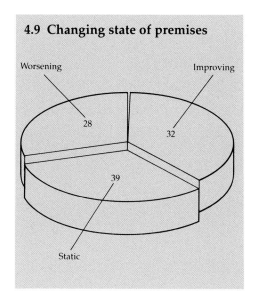

4.9 Changing state of premises

Worsening 28
Improving 32
Static 39

some sort of move, and 26 are either threatened with or have experienced recent loss of space. Over-optimistic forecasts of student numbers in the 1960s have left universities with surplus space, and excessive rates and servicing costs. All Scottish universities have been reallocating space, by amalgamating departments into larger 'cost centres', or by rehousing several departments in accommodation previously designated for one. The Chemistry Department at St Andrews moved into a new building in 1969, by which time student numbers were already falling below the original estimates. In 1975 Geology took over part of the space, and Geography moved in during 1989 causing a further 20 per cent reduction in the Chemistry Department's remaining area. The small Chemistry Museum lost its store in 1979, and will lose two designated museum rooms to Geography, requiring dispersal of the collection, since no provision has been made for it in UGC/UFC space norms. Departmental reorganisation at Dundee has created Applied Physics and Electronic and Manufacturing Engineering (APEME), a unit that replaces three departments, Physics, Electrical Engineering and Mechanical Engineering. APEME is housed in one building, with a foyer area that can now be used to display material from each of its contributory departments.

4.26 Expansion of other facilities may effectively close a museum, as has happened with the Biological Sciences Museum at Stirling and the Natural Philosophy Museum at Aberdeen. Changes in teaching methods led Edinburgh to reduce its collection of gross pathology specimens in 1970 from a two-storey museum to a small mobile cabinet, and to controlled disposal of its Forensic Pathology collection in 1985. Some collections have reaped benefits from change. Glasgow's Pathology Museum holds over 2,000 historical items, including Dr William Hunter's 18th century bone specimens, and equipment and memorabilia associated with the father of modern surgery, Lord Lister. In 1987 pathology teaching space was yielded to the NHS Department of Cytology. Remaining museum space was successfully restructured at the expense of the NHS (who also pay 40 per cent of building running costs) to provide for teaching as well as display, with systematic and historical collections exhibited side by side.

Premises Management

4.27 Except in the eight cases where collections are housed in premises shared with or owned by other organizations such as the NHS, management is invariably in the hands of the Estates and Buildings/Works Department. Some universities now operate an internal accounting system so that departments, including museums, are billed for non-routine services, which can be problematic for collections with no allocated budget. The disadvantages may perhaps be outweighed by the advantages of having ready access to repair services.

4.28 Underfunding of building maintenance inevitably generates a backlog of repairs. At Glasgow, where the university's policy has been to maintain the staff/student ratio in line with UGC recommendations at the expense of fabric maintenance, the Estates and Buildings Officer believes £40 million should be spent across the whole university over the next 10 years to rectify previous neglect. An estimated £250,000 is needed to refurbish the Main Hall of the Hunterian Museum. The UGC Earth Sciences Review will entail alterations to the Geology Department costing some £700,000, to which the UFC will only contribute £500,000 despite the work having been occasioned by its predecessor's recommendations. This does not bode well for due consideration being given to the long-term needs of research collections housed within the department, since storage provision is likely to be sacrificed in such circumstances.

SUMMARY

4.29 In the current economic climate premises are unlikely to be secure for all but the most well-established collections. Though conditions were described as adequate for 56 collections, and as improving for 32, protection is needed for the 17 in poor conditions and the 28 whose circumstances were described as worsening. Recommendations relating to premises, their improvement and restoration, or on the need to secure space during reorganization pro-grammes, were made 14 times in the visit reports, indicating that the current position is less than satisfactory. Information gathered on storage conditions (see para 6.13), which were identified as an area for improvement in a further 16 visit report recommendations, compounds anxiety regarding space provision for university collections.

4.30 It is to be hoped that in future the UFC space norms will allow for collections. Estates and Buildings Officers cannot easily find space when there is no support from the funding body for them to do so. Where a collection has been recognised by the Collections Committee or by an accreditation system such as Registration, it should be entitled to funding and accommodation.

The Hunterian Art Gallery has been able to raise money by royalty payments from Cassina for the reproduction of Mackintosh furniture designs. The chair facing the sideboard is a reproduction of the Argyle Street Tearoom chairs.

5

FINANCE FOR COLLECTIONS, AND POLICY IN FUNDING BODIES

SOURCES OF FUNDS

5.1 Only 31 collections have any sort of allocated budget, while another 31 are dependent on one-off grants from their host department, or occasionally from central university funds. Twenty-nine collections have no funding arrangement of any kind. The main source is implicit support from the UFC's block grant to universities as it filters through uni-

versity space, services and staff costs.

University Grants Committee (UGC)/ Universities Funding Council (UFC)

5.2 As the statutory body for channelling government money to universities, the UFC (successor body to the UGC as from 31 March 1989) necessarily plays an important part in financing collections. It cannot be said to make any direct contribution, since although it has denoted

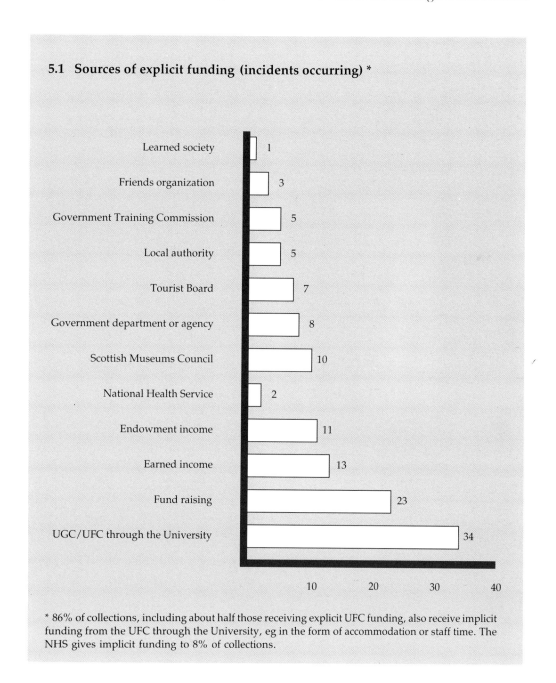

5.1 Sources of explicit funding (incidents occurring) *

Learned society	1
Friends organization	3
Government Training Commission	5
Local authority	5
Tourist Board	7
Government department or agency	8
Scottish Museums Council	10
National Health Service	2
Endowment income	11
Earned income	13
Fund raising	23
UGC/UFC through the University	34

* 86% of collections, including about half those receiving explicit UFC funding, also receive implicit funding from the UFC through the University, eg in the form of accommodation or staff time. The NHS gives implicit funding to 8% of collections.

certain collections as Special Factors, the funds thus allocated have not hitherto been earmarked within the block grant.

5.2 Arrangement of funding (incidents occurring)

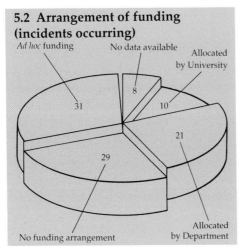

Special Factor Funding

5.3 Special Factor funding, which applies to three Scottish collections (Glasgow's Hunterian Museum and Art Gallery, Aberdeen's Anthropological Museum and Edinburgh's Russell Collection of Early Keyboard Instruments), is awarded from university funds which are calculated according to the following formula:

$$A = T + R(= DR + CR + SR + JR) + S(= NDS + DS)$$

T = teaching resources, related to student numbers; R = research resources; DR = 40 per cent of the income from Research Councils and major charitable bodies; CR = a fraction of £10,000,000, distributed according to the proportion of contract research income from industry and Government Departments; SR = floor provision: an unspecified proportion (thus, an unknown quantity) of the grant determined by weighted student numbers; JR = resources selectively distributed on judgement (thus, a second unknown quantity); S = allowances for non-departmental special factors (NDS) and departmental special factors (DS): these are exceptional commitments, other than for teaching and research, such as museums. Several of these

elements are unknown quantities, as is the position of the new UFC on Special Factor funding. Insufficient information is available to assess either past practice or future direction.

5.4 Theoretically the Special Factor should protect a museum against financial cutbacks, and though detailed accounts cannot be extracted for UGC/UFC investment in Scotland's Special Factor funded museums, it does appear to have done so to a limited extent. From 1984–85 to 1989–90, the Hunterian Museum has seen its non-salary budget keep reasonably in step with the overall funding of the University of Glasgow. The Anthropological Museum has been totally redisplayed since 1987 while the rest of the University of Aberdeen has been in financial crisis. However this was funded through the University's Development Fund, not from UGC sources, and has not prevented staff losses. The Russell Collection has been able to maintain its services, and to expand the amount of time the Curator spends on the collection from 13 to 20 hours per week, but we cannot know what the UGC/UFC's contribution has been. Again, we cannot extract detailed accounts for UGC investment in the museum, but the implication is that Special Factor funding has protected the museum to some extent.

5.5 The attitude of the UFC to the Special Factor policy established by its predecessor is unclear, though there is likely to be some shift in overall strategy. The title change from University Grants Committee to Universities Funding Council implies increased emphasis on non-governmental money, which is already a feature in the many plural-funded university collections. According to the UFC's 1991–95 prospectus, universities will henceforth bid for prospective student numbers in different subjects, with the target 'price' for each student being set by the UFC. Research funding will be distributed by a reward system according to the results of the recent research selectivity exercise. Universities are being encouraged to recruit more non-standard students, to offer more relevant and flexible courses, to collaborate more closely with industry, business and the professions, and to operate more managerially. It is to be hoped that these changes may enable the UFC to be more informative than the UGC as to the awarding of funds and the significance of Special Factor status.

5.6 The Committee of Vice-Chancellors and Principals has added its voice to calls on the UFC to extend its support for university collections, requesting that *additional* funding be made available to the UFC to enable the Council to provide increased funding selectively to a larger number of museums and galleries which the (Museums and Galleries) Commission identifies as eligible for special factor funding'.[4] There are certainly more collections in Scotland than the three Special Factor funded museums which have material meeting the UGC's criterion of activities which might be at risk because costs are above average, but which should be retained in the national interest. Selective funding could however be prejudicial to the bulk of collections, many incorporating items of international significance. Natural Science collections in all the universities hold type and figured material which must be retained and curated for reference purposes. Yet they are outside the likely remit of Special Factor funding. Such collections need to be brought to the attention of funding bodies through committee representation to their university, and thence to the UFC.

UGC Subject Reviews

5.7 The UGC undertook a number of subject reviews which, though making little reference to collections, have affected their administration. The UFC has decided not to carry out any more subject reviews, and is not to enforce the recommendations of reviews performed but not yet implemented, leaving universities themselves to make strategic plans for individual subjects. The linked Chemistry and Physics Reviews, which fall into this category, made no allowance for interesting and important material at St Andrews, Glasgow, Aberdeen, Dundee and Strathclyde. Despite the recent announcement, universities have already reacted to the detriment of collections: the Chemistry Museum at St Andrews is to be disbanded; the Kelvin Collection at Glasgow is to lose its present display area; the Natural Philosophy collection at Aberdeen is to go into store; and the chemistry and physics collections at Dundee and Strathclyde face uncertain futures.

UGC Earth Sciences Review

5.8 Though the completion of the Earth Sciences Review was announced in 1987, few departments knew what their future was to hold until March 1988, when restructuring for October 1989 began. In Scotland, Edinburgh and Glasgow were identified as Type M, providing teaching and research in mainstream earth sciences, Aberdeen and St Andrews were made smaller departments offering joint honours and service teaching, while Dundee and Strathclyde were closed altogether. Under a tight schedule, a Museums and Collections Committee chaired by Sir Alwyn Williams was required to report to the UGC on the distribution and resourcing of collections, their future pattern of distribution, and arrangements (including relocation) for ensuring that the museum function was properly considered in reorganisation. Following the UGC's failure to endorse this report, the five proposed Collection

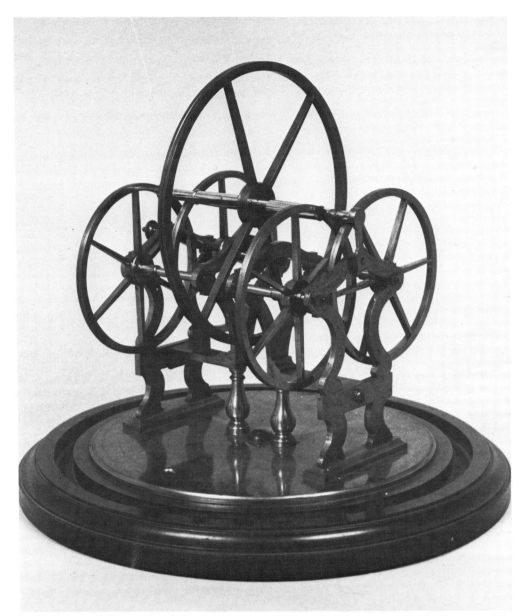

Superb workmanship in a set of friction wheels formerly on top of an Atwood's Machine. The wheels are attributed by College records to the hand of the instrument-making Professor Patrick Copland in the late eighteenth century. (Natural Philosophy Collection, Aberdeen.)

Centres, of which Glasgow's Hunterian Museum is one, were invited to submit bids for the likely costs of transfer and maintenance of the enlarged collections. Two experts were informally charged by the UGC with assessing these bids for one-off expenditure and recurrent costs. The UFC response will apparently involve new money, and will not indicate cutbacks on present funding for university collections. UFC financial support (albeit not yet formally proffered) will help to unlock other grants. For example, the SMC sees the distribution of those

collections as falling within the scope of the reorganization of natural science collections recommended in the Miles Report (MGC, 1986), and is prepared to grant-aid provision of the necessary geological storage.

UGC/UFC Provision for Collections

5.9 In the past the UGC did make specific provision for collections, as the Wright Report described:

... information obtained by the Standing Commission shows that UGC money has recently been available for a number of museums' capital projects, particularly where a Departmental museum is to be housed in a new Departmental building which UGC is financing, but the UGC unfortunately has not felt able to accept full responsibility for those university museums not solely concerned with teaching within the university (DES, 1973).

The Biological Sciences Museum at Stirling was a capital project funded on this basis by the UGC (see para 1.5).

5.10 Future involvement could be responsive to advice from parties concerned with university collections, such as the MGC, the Committee of Vice-Chancellors and Principals, the UMG and UMIS and the Area Museum Councils. Issues such as Special Factor funding for museums, and possibilities for satisfactory ways of supporting the bulk of worthy university collections, could be examined by a group of advisors. UFC support for the Northern England University Collections Survey is a welcome instance of more generalised assistance which could be maintained throughout the planned national programme of surveys.

Museums and Galleries Commission (MGC)

5.11 The Commission has grant-aided all the university collections research projects to date. It has also made conservation grants to Scottish university collections in the past, and a Registration scheme compatible with the one it is now running in England should be adopted in Scotland in 1990–91, subject to Scottish Office consent.

Government Training Agencies

5.12 Before the change from MSC to ET

schemes in 1988, there was a high level of investment in university collections (see paras 4.14, 4.15). The Community Programme Unit which remodelled Edinburgh's Zoology Museum employed 13 staff and had an associated materials and costs budget, amounting to total MSC expenditure of £60,500 in 1987–88. Until 1988, one-third of the Hunterian Museum and Art Gallery's overall funding came from the MSC.

Scottish Education Department (SED)

5.13 SED is the sponsoring department for the SMC. In its response to the Miles Report (MGC, 1986), it authorised the SMC to use its grant-in-aid to support the establishment of SUCRU, and undertook to draw the Report's other recommendations on university collections to the attention of those concerned.[5] SED funding for the NMS NAPIER project is likely to prove valuable to university collections, firstly on account of the service's advisory remit, and secondly in the possibilities it raises for including data on university collections in the overall documentation of Scottish museum collections (see para 6.20). The National Fund for Acquisition—Scotland (formerly the Local Museums Purchase Fund), administered by the NMS on behalf of the SED, is increasingly stretched, so that it sometimes meets 15 per cent rather than 50 per cent of purchase cost, but it has proved valuable to established museums.

Scottish Development Department (SDD)

5.14 SDD has had some impact on university collections by funding archaeological research on excavated skeletal remains at Aberdeen's Anatomy Department, and through excavation grants awarded to the Hunterian Museum and the Marine Archaeology Institute at St Andrews. Its Artefact Research Unit has made occasional use of Edinburgh's Archaeology Teaching Collection, and its Finds Disposal Panel recognizes certain university archaeological museums as recipients for excavated material and makes a modest, one-off payment towards storage costs.

Scottish Tourist Board (STB)

5.15 STB has made grants to the Hunterian Museum and Art Gallery, the Anthropological Museum and the Collins Gallery. It provides useful marketing advice and support, but extensive involvement is proscribed by the specific conditions attached to Section 4 grants. In 1988 the UMG was addressed by Robert Jackson, Under Secretary of State with responsibility for Higher Education, who suggested that university museums should market themselves better as tourist attractions and as candidates for local authority grants and commercial sponsorship. However, as the Minister for Tourism had pointed out to the UMG Chairman at a previous meeting, Section 4 grants for tourism are available for capital costs for new projects but not for running costs, and so are of limited use to established collections. Moreover, STB now requires museums to open on weekends during six summer months, which few universities can afford.

Scottish Development Agency (SDA)

5.16 The SDA's Conservation Bureau provides an important focal point for conservation in Scotland. Recently reactivated by the appointment of a conservation officer in 1989, its advisory services and grant-aid programmes are available to university collections in Scotland.

Area Museum Councils

5.17 Area Museum Councils have heightened awareness of the plight of university collections. In 1983–84 the Area Museums Service for South Eastern England surveyed the University of London's collections, and separately, in less detail, university museums in South Eastern England (Bass, 1984b). In 1986 the East Midlands Area Museum Service looked at the three universities in its area,[6] and in 1989 the London Museums Service made a further study of London's collections (Arnold-Forster, 1989). The Scottish university collections project began in 1988 under the auspices of the SMC (see paras 1.17, 1.18), and is being followed by a Northern England survey jointly administered by the North West Museum and Art Gallery Service, the North of England Museums Service and the Area Museum and Art Gallery Service for Yorkshire and Humberside. An analogous exercise is being considered by the Area Museum Council for the South West. As the MGC has asked all Area Councils to survey university collections in their area (MGC, 1987), their involvement looks set to grow over the next few years.

Local Authority Funding

5.18 The level of local authority funding remains low despite the Miles Report's (MGC, 1986) recommendation of greater input by local authorities, echoed by the MGC (MGC, 1987). Historic rivalry between town and gown is being broken down as universities seek to develop community links and as local authorities recognize the multiplier effect of the microeconomy in their midst. However in major cities like Dundee, Glasgow, Edinburgh and Aberdeen (where all Scottish universities except Stirling and St Andrews are located), local government at District level already has a

Hunterian Museum, University of Glasgow. A Wealth of Nations. *To left: William Hunter with documents relating to his coin collection. Centre: The heads of all the Roman Emperors are portrayed on gold* aurei *and* solidi. *Right: Other Roman coins celebrating gods and goddesses, public works and victories. The tribute money (Matthew 22:21) is shown by itself. The panel above explains the inscriptions on Roman Coins. Scottish Museum of the Year Award, 1984.*

substantial commitment to museums. The City of Glasgow District Council supports ten museums, among them Glasgow Art Gallery and Museum, the Burrell Collection, the Transport Museum, the People's Palace Museum and the Botanic Gardens. In the last 12 years the City of Glasgow District Council's grant to the Hunterian Museum and Art Gallery has amounted to just £7,000. It has however agreed to fund weekend opening during the summer of 1990, Glasgow's year as European City of Culture.

5.19 Instances of co-operation do exist, such as the plan to establish a conservation service shared between the Anthropological Museum, Aberdeen University Library and Aberdeen Art Gallery and Museums (see para 6.9). Local government legislation in Scotland implicitly requires District Councils to make adequate museum provision, and this is presumably what has encouraged North-East Fife District Council Museums Service to accept material from the erstwhile Archaeological Museum at St Andrews with a view to opening its own museum in the town. Local authorities are developing museum services, which discourages them from passing local material over to central repositories like the Archaeology Department of the Hunterian Museum, and which leaves little leeway for supporting external collections. However as the SMC suggested in its written evidence to the MGC's Working Party on Local Authorities and Museums (SMC, 1989), this may also be a strength in that professional staff are available within local museum services to offer advice to curators and Collections Committees in universities.

Educational Departments of Regional Councils

5.20 Reluctance by the Education Departments of Regional Councils to support educational activities in university museums has been overcome at the Hunterian Museum where Strathclyde Regional Council gives the University £12,000 per year in recognition of the local function of the museum's schools service, and now provides a teacher, but it remains a source of frustration to the Curator of the Anthropological Museum at Aberdeen. Despite a programme which involved 2,700 primary schoolchildren visiting the museum to attend classes taken by curators (1987–88), use of the museum by the Urban Studies Centre which sends schools there as part of an educational package, and a comprehensive set of worksheets and teachers' notes distributed by the museum, Grampian Regional Council has refused to fund a museum education officer post, or to provide a seconded teacher. In view of the fact that such educational activities are estimated to take up 15 per cent of curatorial time, the university is currently making a sizeable hidden contribution to local education services.

Fund-raising and Sponsorship

5.21 Many collections have managed to raise funds from sponsorship, through Friends' organizations, or by merchandising their collections. We have noted 51 instances where collections generate income from private sector sources. The Hunterian Art Gallery is a model for this approach, since by selling duplicate prints, by royalty arrangements on Cassina replicas of furniture by C. R. Mackintosh, by charging fees for conferences and functions held in the galleries, by entrance fees for afternoon visitors to Mackintosh House and by donation, it has accumulated an endowment fund of some £250,000. Few collections have the advantage of assets like Mackintosh and Whistler, but examples of inventive fund-raising abound. The Russell Collection of Early Keyboard Instruments in Edinburgh makes money from the sale of patterns for instruments, books and records while the Peto Collection in Dundee raises some £1,000 per year from use of its photographs by publishers, television companies and exhibitions. Collections which have Friends' organizations, such as the Reid Collection of Historic Musical Instruments and the Russell Collection, have benefited substantially from their help in raising money. Entry charges are rare. The Robertson Museum and Aquarium which is jointly owned by the Universities of Glasgow and London makes a small charge, as does the Hunterian Art Gallery for afternoon visits to Mackintosh House.

5.22 Sponsorship is notoriously time-consuming, so it is rarely a useful source of revenue for collections without at least part-time salaried staff. Corporate fund-raising through committees who can then distribute money to their constituent collections may be a way of overcoming this difficulty. Strathclyde's Collins Gallery currently has sponsorship for 10 per cent of its exhibition budget, and the Curator intends to raise the proportion to 50 per cent by 1990–91, amounting to some £50,000. An attractive exhibition programme, a full-time Curator with administrative support and £10,000 from Strathclyde's *Advisory Group on Cultural Activities* (£2,000 of which has been passed over in advance to pay for marketing to sponsors and a new corporate image for the gallery) all make this ambition achievable. Sponsorship for care of collections, and for essential staff resources is by contrast all but impossible to find.

5.23 Charitable trusts have been a source of some revenue. SUCRU has been sponsored by the MacRobert Trusts and the Carnegie Trust for the Universities of Scotland. From 1985–89, the Radcliffe, Mathew and Pilgrim Trusts awarded a total of £43,800 to fund the training of a Conservator and to carry out archive conservation in the University Library at Dundee. The Hunterian Art Gallery has had assistance from the Pilgrim Trust, the National Art Collections Fund, the National Heritage Memorial Fund, the Henry Moore Foundation and the Scottish Arts Council—a good example of targeted fund-raising.

SUMMARY

5.24 Although the level of explicit funding from universities to collections is disappointingly low, curators have been ingenious in their pursuit of alternative sources of money. Plural funding is highly developed, with collections owned by the University of Glasgow tapping all twelve categories of funding, and those in universities with less sophisticated organizational structures still showing acumen in accessing the majority of them. However, efficient collections management and forward planning are hampered in the 60 collections with no allocated budget, meaning that hard-earned income may be unwittingly dissipated.

5.25 It is to be hoped that universities and their sponsoring body the UFC, might, on the advice of University Collections Committees, award more funding for Designated Collections, that local authorities might accord university collections more recognition of their educational role, and that Collections Committees might be able to raise funds corporately to the benefit of all collections under their auspices.

The high density geology storage system at St Andrews was inherited from the University Library. Sited in the basement of the Department of Geology, it replaces various unsatisfactory scattered off-site stores.

6 CARE OF COLLECTIONS

CONSERVATION

6.1 In situations where resources are stretched, and where curators are inadequately trained in care of collections, conservation is invariably accorded low priority and objects are liable to be damaged by unsatisfactory environmental conditions or inappropriate handling. That the overall state of collections is largely described as good/adequate testifies more to the technical care previously available for university collections than to any current conservation activity. Conservation was cited as a priority area for improvement in 31 visit reports, focusing on the need for professional assessment, for conservation plans, and for the application of preventative care and remedial treatment. Only documentation was instanced more frequently. However, in 42 cases no development of the potential for conservation was thought likely.

6.1 Overall state of collections

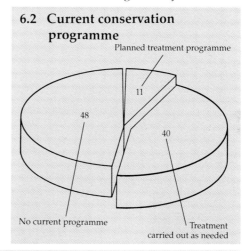

6.2 Current conservation programme

6.3 Limitations to development of conservation (instances occurring)

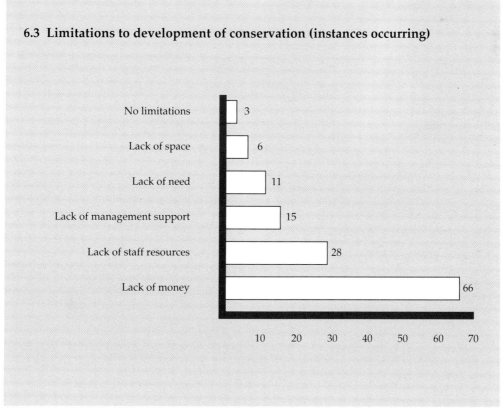

Causes of deterioration

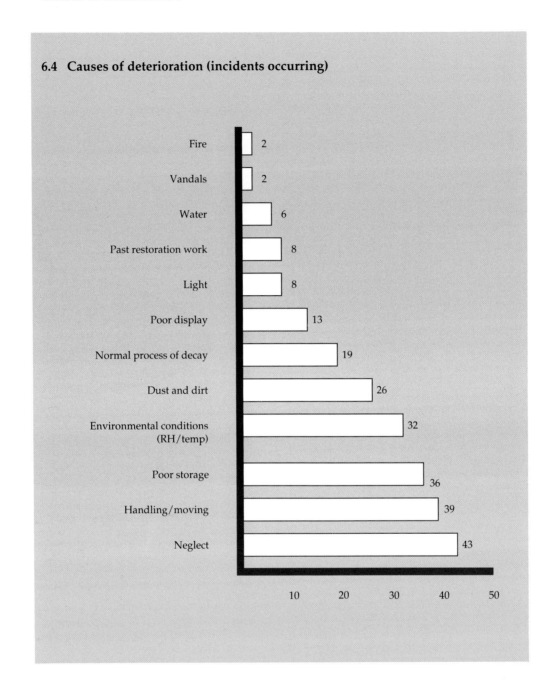

6.4 Causes of deterioration (incidents occurring)

Fire	2
Vandals	2
Water	6
Past restoration work	8
Light	8
Poor display	13
Normal process of decay	19
Dust and dirt	26
Environmental conditions (RH/temp)	32
Poor storage	36
Handling/moving	39
Neglect	43

6.2 Our data show that the predominant causes of deterioration are those relating to lack of good housekeeping rather than to faulty intervention. Poor control of relative humidity and temperature fluctuation, together with poor storage conditions, are compounded by damage from handling that occurs when collections of delicate material are moved. However, training of curators and improved awareness of the needs of collections at curatorial and management levels would reduce the damaging effects of such disruption.

6.3 The prime cause of deterioration is neglect, both past and present. This can best be alleviated in the short term by training curators in preventative conservation, and in the long-term by instituting systems of curatorial control through the University Curator and a Collections Committee.

Preventative conservation

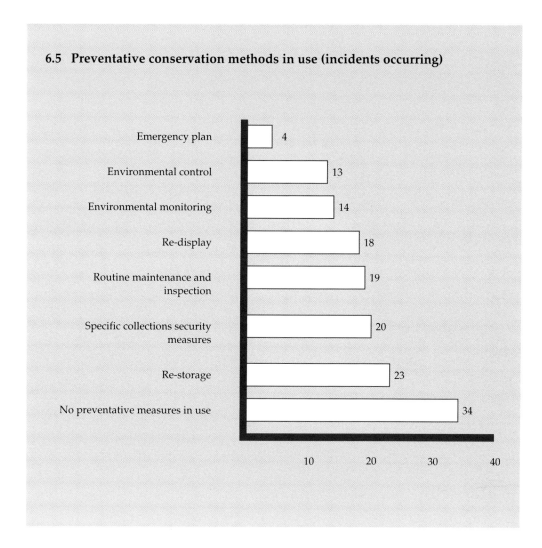

6.5 Preventative conservation methods in use (incidents occurring)

Emergency plan	4
Environmental control	13
Environmental monitoring	14
Re-display	18
Routine maintenance and inspection	19
Specific collections security measures	20
Re-storage	23
No preventative measures in use	34

6.4 Preventative conservation is at a low level. Thirty-four collections are applying no such measures, and it is disturbing to find that only four collections have any sort of emergency plan; these tend to be collections held within libraries. The lack of environmental monitoring (14 instances) and of routine maintenance and inspection (19 instances) are evidence of poor housekeeping.

6.5 The remedies are as above; training for curators, and a more organized network of responsibility for collections. Preventative conservation requires time for routine good housekeeping and collection care which must be allowed for by university management. Since over 50 per cent of collections are curated by staff who spend less than 10 per cent of their time on them, resources are spread very thinly indeed.

Remedial Conservation Treatment

6.6 Lack of money, the most frequently cited limitation to development in conservation, restricts access to professional treatment and advice, while lack of contact with the museum profession hampers collections in tapping available sources of grant-aid and treatment. Forty-eight collections have no current programme of conservation treatment.

6.7 Private conservators are the most

6.6 Recourse to remedial conservation treatment

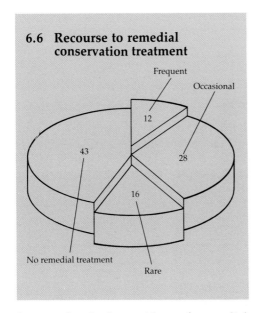

frequently cited providers of remedial treatment. Only four conservators are employed within the eight Scottish universities. Despite its national status and the acknowledged excellence of its exhibition and educational work, the Hunterian Museum (as distinct from the Art Gallery) does not employ a conservator and spent a mere £300 on remedial conservation in 1988–89, out of an allocated budget of £29,000, though approximately £3,000 per year is available for grant-aided preventative conservation measures such as improved storage.

6.8 At St Andrews, the University Court on the recommendation of the Finance and Resources Committee makes an annual allocation of £1,000 for conservation. However, the costly treatment of the split-second clock by Joseph Knibb (1677) has resulted in the mortgaging of the conservation budget. The programme for the two matching longcase clocks by Knibb, for which the SMC has offered 50 per cent matching grant-aid, is now in jeopardy. The budget is therefore inadequate to cover the real cost of conservation treatment for collections throughout the university.

Meeting the Cost of Conservation by Co-operative Ventures

6.9 The cost of conservation can be spread by co-operation between institutions with similar requirements. At Aberdeen, a proposal is currently being considered to set up a conservation service meeting the needs of the University Library, the Anthropological Museum and Aberdeen Art Gallery and Museum. In the long run, such a service could generate income by accepting work from outside clients. The University Library at Dundee is seeking funds to enlarge its archive conservation service so that it can do work for outside institutions and individuals. Co-operation between the SMC and the University of Edinburgh's General Council

6.7 Providers of remedial conservation treatment (incidents occurring)

External	
Service provided by another museum	1
Non-specialist	1
Scottish Museums Council conservation services	11
Private conservators	17

Internal	
Miscellaneous (volunteers, MSC/ET)	3
Professional conservator	8
Curator	12
Technician	17

One of a pair of longcase clocks made by Joseph Knibb about 1673 for the mathematician-astronomer James Gregory, Professor of Mathematics at St Andrews; he also commissioned a bracket clock for measuring one-third seconds, possibly the first clock to read to the accuracy of a fraction of a second.

has provided funding to employ a conservator for an initial period of one year in the newly refurbished Zoology Museum.

Problems Arising from the Loss of Technical Posts

6.10 The position regarding conservation is perhaps not as bad as it might be, because many curators are informally helped by skilled technicians who have the expertise to repair scientific instruments or to look after specimens in their discipline. However, loss of technical posts over the last ten years has reduced available time for remedial and preventative treatment; the research technologist who curated and conserved the Kelvin collection at Glasgow died in 1983 and was not replaced. As a 1988 SMC Conservation Survey reported (SMC, 1988):

> The collection is reasonably well-documented, catalogued, and is visited by an international audience; it would be tragic if all the hard work and care of past curators were to be lost because the wherewithal for basic maintenance could not now be found.

Scientific Instruments

6.11 Scientific instruments, which occur in 37 university collections, are comparatively rare outside universities, so it is worrying that they are likely to be so unaffected by preventative or professional conservation. They are particularly vulnerable to damage from inexperienced handling and frequent moves. Being housed in the departments most affected by space reallocation plans such as Physics and Chemistry, they are therefore much at risk. *A Conservation Survey of Museum Collections in Scotland* (Ramer, 1989) found that:

> Poor maintenance and inadequate storage space are the critical factors

which adversely affect the scientific instrument collections. Without a regular programme of maintenance, items are undergoing slow deterioration due to the accumulation of surface dust and dirt. With respect to storage, the periodic movement of objects into increasingly diminished space is a potential cause of increased damage.

As the survey notes, the remedial needs of such collections could largely be met by suitably trained technical staff, working within the context of a planned conservation programme. Agencies concerned with conservation practice and training, such as the SMC and the Conservation Bureau (SDA), might take particular note of the conservation needs of scientific instrument collections within universities.

Conservation Planning

6.12 Conservation planning, with professional assessment of the priority needs and costs of preventative and remedial treatment over several years, would, when combined with an identified budget, enable universities to improve the state of their collections. At present only 11 collections work within such a plan. The SMC, already a significant source of advice and financial support for conservation in university collections, awarding £20,054 in 50 per cent matching grants for remedial conservation to universities in 1989, is able to provide guidance in these areas.

STORAGE

6.13 Although 37 collections are housed in purpose-built storage, and 41 are in suitable space, poor quality housing and insecurity of storage space contribute to collection damage. Thirty-four collec-

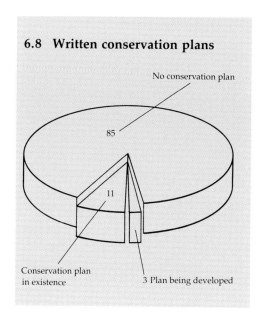

6.8 Written conservation plans

No conservation plan

85

11

Conservation plan in existence

3 Plan being developed

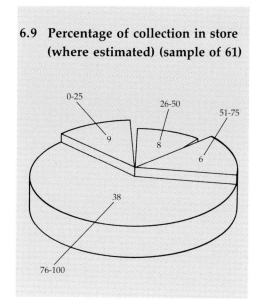

6.9 Percentage of collection in store (where estimated) (sample of 61)

0-25

26-50

51-75

9

8

6

38

76-100

tions have 90 per cent or more of their material in store: of these 16 have no material on display at all. In such circumstances, adequate provision is essential. In 45 instances, however, it is thought unlikely that improved or additional storage will be developed.

The Implications of Space Rationalization Programmes

6.14 Space rationalization has cut storage capacity, though new money may be forthcoming to mitigate some difficulties (see para 5.8). Delicate materials like botanical specimens or scientific instruments are sensitive to vibration and excessive handling brought about by frequent moves. Due to space shortages, historical objects may be stored with equipment in current use. The Natural Philosophy collections in Aberdeen and St Andrews are housed in lecture preparation rooms, where they are categorized according to function and are not separated from contemporary items regularly used for demonstration.

The Effect of Written Collecting Policies

6.15 Written policies are needed to con-

trol the growth of collections which might otherwise exhaust available storage space. Nothing could be worse for material that *is* worthy of retention than that it should come to be seen as part of a bulk storage problem. Discrimination between objects should ensure that only enough material as can be managed effectively is retained. Rapid turnover in scientific equipment is generating many potential museum objects. Even where a pre-accession disposal policy is operated, as with Glasgow's History of Science collection, growth rate (in the period 1986–88 the collection doubled in size) may require strategic intervention.

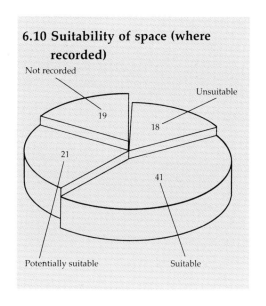

6.10 Suitability of space (where recorded)

Not recorded

Unsuitable

19

18

21

41

Potentially suitable

Suitable

When developing written collecting policies, curators should assess their university's ability to store material against a projected growth rate.

Central Storage Repositories

6.16 Some subjects, particularly those where collections are integral to research, have a built-in growth factor which has not been accounted for in UFC space norms, though implied UFC support for bulk storage for collections accruing to the Hunterian Museum as a result of the UGC's Earth Sciences review is an encouraging sign of awareness that such needs exist (see para 5.8). Arnold-Forster's study of London's collections (Arnold-Forster, 1989) recommends that the university consider developing an off-site central repository. This may be the sensible solution for universities whose premises are becoming choked with seldom-used research material. Rising space costs make the option of off-site high density storage look economically attractive. Such storage needs

regular supervision and environmental monitoring which should be carried out by a suitably trained curator. Universities might be able to arrange joint storage with local museums, as is being investigated at present for the Natural History Collections of the University of Glasgow and of the City Museum and Art Gallery, though supervisory arrangements must be negotiated and collections should be adequately documented prior to installation. A further possibility, of subcontracting storage to an archiving company, may prove cost-efficient in terms of staff and space overheads where security combined with infrequent need for access is the main consideration.

DOCUMENTATION

6.17 In two-thirds of collections (65 instances) development or improvement of documentation was seen as a possibility. The need to continue and extend current documentation programmes and to develop computerised and compatible systems led documentation to be cited 36

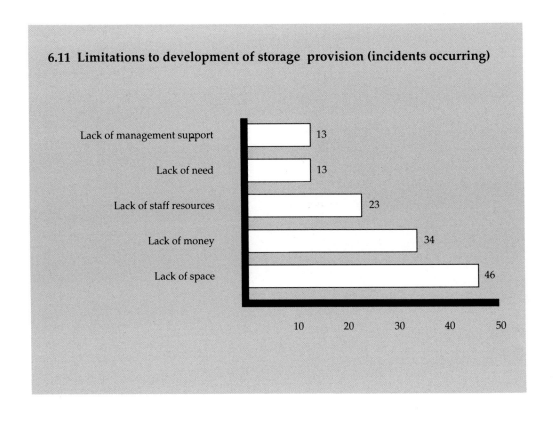

6.11 Limitations to development of storage provision (incidents occurring)

6.12 Documentation systems in use in 85 collections (incidents occurring) *

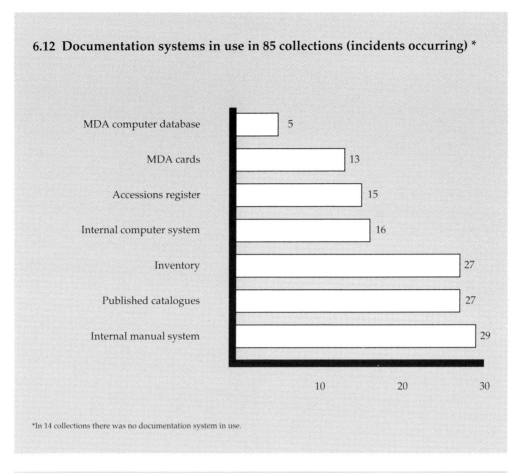

*In 14 collections there was no documentation system in use.

6.13 Limitations to development of documentation (incidents occurring)

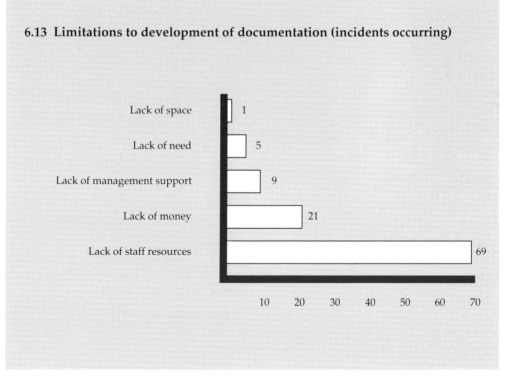

times as a priority recommendation in visit reports. Documentation is the most efficient mechanism for managing collections, so it is to be hoped that these recommendations will influence curators and management.

Systems and Standards

6.18 Documentation standards vary widely, even within collections. Curators may only be able to tackle documentation in their spare time — lack of staff resources is recorded as the prime factor in limiting development of documentation (69 instances). Curators may be unfamiliar with the systems commonly used in museums, such as the Museum Documentation Association (MDA) cards or computer data-base, which have only been applied in 18 cases. Self-devised systems, not necessarily compatible with the MDA system, are much more common, occurring in 45 instances. Attempts to regularize documentation have been hampered by the cessation of MSC schemes in 1988. As a result cataloguing has slowed drastically, with the long-term prospect of a mounting backlog of unrecorded material in all universities.

Risks Associated with Inadequate Documentation

6.19 Lack of continuity in curatorship leaves documentation prone to inconsistency and incompleteness, and the 14 collections listed as operating no system at all reflect incidents where knowledge of an entire collection may be held in the memory of one interested person. An undocumented collection is unprotected from disposal or dispersal, having no identified integrity. It is especially at risk during space reallocation, for without the testimonial of a written record of its contents, a collection may be seen simply as a waste of space for which no one is willing to accept responsibility.

Data Gathered by the Scottish University Collections Research Unit

6.20 Data gathered during the process of this survey, which have been logged at the NMS, merely indicate the wealth and breadth of collections. This points to a possible second stage for the project—development of a full-scale documentation programme for university collections throughout Scotland in association with the NMS NAPIER project. Such a programme would be valuable to universities and museums, particularly if the data were compatible with those in other universities and museums in Britain.

SUMMARY AND POTENTIAL DEVELOPMENTS

6.21 Collections care is at a low level in universities. Some shining exceptions exist such as the Hunterian Art Gallery where there has been enough money to instal a high-quality compact storage system and to employ a trained conservator. When resources are scarce, curators are naturally inclined to concentrate on 'front-of-house' activities at the expense of support services, with damaging long-term consequences for objects.

6.22 Predictably the fundamental problem is lack of resources of staff, time, money and space. Access to SMC conservation services (currently under review), and indeed to professional conservation whatever its source, is limited by the costs involved. Preventative conservation needs commitment from curators and their employers to training and regular collection monitoring which cannot be guaranteed under present constraints on staffing. Poor storage conditions and inconsistent documentation make collection control more difficult, adding to the long-term costs and risks of loss from deterioration or disposal.

6.23 Universities should recognize the urgent need for improvements to conservation, storage and documentation, and should contribute to the costs of operating appropriate policies and systems. Care of collections is an area where co-operative initiatives are particularly appropriate, seen for example in the planned joint University/City Museum and Art Gallery conservation service in Aberdeen, the possibilities for combined storage being discussed by the Hunterian Museum and Glasgow Museum and Art Gallery, and the potential for a documentation programme capable of handling information from all the Scottish university collections.

View of display from "Brass Roots: 150 Years of Brass Bands", a touring exhibition mounted jointly in 1989–90 by the University of Edinburgh and Bradford Museums and Art Galleries.

RESEARCH

7.1 Our data show that university staff are making use of collections for research in 64 instances in all, and that 44 collections are attracting outside researchers. Collections are therefore playing a significant part in current research programmes which goes largely unrecognized by university management and funding bodies. Since research success is an important factor in generating university income, it is disappointing that in 67 instances no development of the use of collections for research is thought likely; lack of staff resources is the prime factor limiting development of this area (48 instances).

The Use of Collections in Certain Subjects

7.2 Some subjects require collections for research, for example earth sciences, botany, archaeology and aspects of zoology, anthropology, geography and music. All type and figured specimens must be curated adequately in the interests of research, and there are sufficient such examples in Scottish universities to make the lack of provision for collection care disturbing in an international context. Anatomy, pathology, forensic science, dental anatomy and veterinary anatomy make less use of gross speci-

mens now than in the past, the principal thrust of research being cellular and subcellular, but they are still necessary for certain lines of investigation. Historical pathological specimens are a way to study advanced forms of diseases which nowadays rarely occur in the western world, and new radiographic imaging techniques are reviving interest among radiologists in cross-sectional anatomy. Scientists at the University of California at Berkeley have retrieved intact sequences of DNA from the dried tissues of nearly 100 mummified corpses, using a technique called the polymerase chain reaction which can now be used to study the genetic evolution of species. As the Earth Sciences Review has shown, the UGC/UFC has so far only recognized the research value of collections when prompted to do so by curators and such professional bodies as the Geological Curators Group. There is no indication that the UFC has accounted for work on collections in its recent research selectivity exercise, details of which were released in Summer 1989 (THES, 1.9.89). Such lack of recognition is reflected in the universities themselves. Research into historic collections seldom receives credit, being seen as peripheral to predominant research orientation. However, physicists in Aberdeen and St Andrews have published articles on the history of science, as have physiologists,

7.1 Use of collections in research (incidents occurring)*

	Frequent	Occasional	Rare	Total	percentage of 73
University staff	30	24	10	64	88%
University students	19	12	8	39	53%
Outside researchers	11	23	10	44	60%

*In 26 collections no use was made of the collections in research.

medical scientists, research technologists and others working on university collections.

Factors Limiting Research Development

7.3 Potential research developments are hampered by lack of staff time to undertake work on collections, to supervise research students, or to improve access by spreading information beyond the confines of the individual university. The SMC's study of *Aberdeen University Museums* (SMC, 1986b) made the following point with reference to acquisition unguided by a collecting policy:

> Material is acquired passively.... There is no tendency to build on strengths or fill gaps in coverage (except in the latter case for small numbers of items for teaching purposes). Staff involved with the museum collections are therefore not motivated with a definite aim in view.

Similarly, the lack of a highly developed collection in specific groups reduces the chances of attracting researchers to Aberdeen. The museum collections do not themselves generate research within the university which they could be capable of if developed.

Though the study was reviewing natural science collections, Edinburgh's Russell Collection of Early Keyboard Instruments confirms the point by contrast. Here public entrance is deliberately restricted in order to allow musicians and researchers to use a 'live' museum, where within certain restrictions instruments can be played. This *is* a collection highly developed in a specific area, and it *does* attract researchers.

Developing Collections for Their Long-Term Research Interest

7.4 Deliberate development of a collection for its long-term research interest is unusually farsighted. One example is the

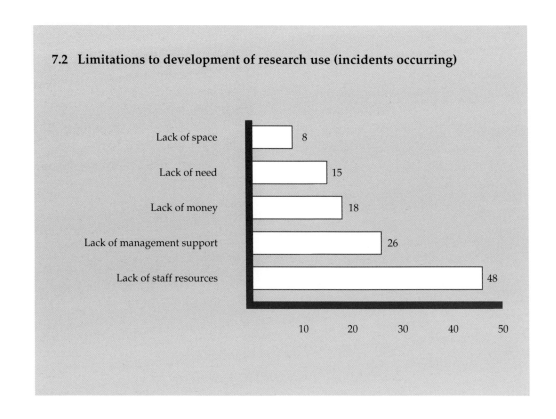

7.2 Limitations to development of research use (incidents occurring)

Lack of space	8
Lack of need	15
Lack of money	18
Lack of management support	26
Lack of staff resources	48

7.3 Use of collections in education (incidents occurring)*

	Frequent	Occasional	Rare	Total	Percentage of 73
Undergraduates in the related department	31	14	8	53	73%
Undergraduates in various departments	9	8	2	19	26%
Extra Mural classes	4	7		11	15%
Open University teaching	4	5		9	12%
Schools	21	17		38	52%
Interested groups	4	7	1	12	16%

*26 collections were not used for education.

Historical Medical Ultrasound Equipment collection at Glasgow's Queen Mother's Hospital, an initiative supported by the Hospital, by Glasgow's Department of Midwifery, by the Hunterian Museum, and by the British Medical Ultrasound Society. The collection of equipment and archive material places diagnostic ultrasound not only in the context of the hospital where it was pioneered by Professor Ian Donald's team in the mid 1950s, but also in that of medical history. It would be unfortunate if universities were unable to provide facilities for such collections, which illustrate the history of the university, and give an evolutionary perspective which may inform future research and development.

EDUCATION

7.5 Collections are being used for undergraduate teaching in a total of 72 instances, for further education in 20 instances (with 12 more citations for use by interested groups) and for schools in 38 instances. The figures for undergraduate teaching imply that use extends further into departmental and university collections than has hitherto been realised, since only 30 collections have been specifically described as teaching collections. In two-thirds of the collections visited (64 instances) no development of the educational use of the collections was thought likely.

Educational services provided

7.6 Our evidence suggests that despite the lack of special staff for educational services, collections play an essential part in normal undergraduate teaching (in 49 cases), and that university curators are devoting considerable energies to running guided tours, loan collections and special lectures for visitors (57 instances). The damaging effects of low staff resources, by far the most frequently cited limitation to development of educational use (55 instances), seem to have been minimised by the efforts of university curators.

Educational Outreach Work

7.7 Any accusation that university collections exist in ivory towers remote from their local community can be rebutted by evidence of their use at all school levels, in further education, and by special interest groups.

Educational Work with Schools

7.8 School curricular changes are proceeding apace in Scotland, with investigative work being emphasised for all ages. Initiatives like the Primary Education Development Project include a significant component of environmental awareness (locality, history etc), which will lead to further demands on

7.4 Limitations to development of educational use of collections (incidents occurring)

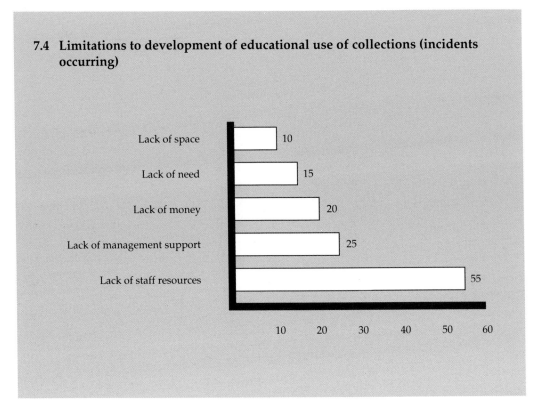

Lack of space — 10
Lack of need — 15
Lack of money — 20
Lack of management support — 25
Lack of staff resources — 55

10 20 30 40 50 60

7.5 Educational services provided (incidents occurring)

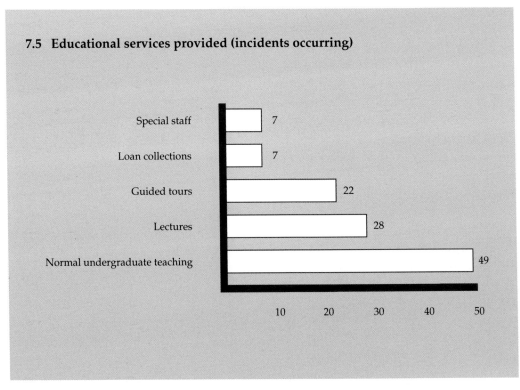

Special staff — 7
Loan collections — 7
Guided tours — 22
Lectures — 28
Normal undergraduate teaching — 49

10 20 30 40 50

museums. Curators are capable of meeting such demands if they are adequately recompensed by a Regional Education Authority, and by their employers and the UFC. The Hunterian Museum and Art Gallery is the only university museum with a teacher funded by a Regional Council, who provides a crucial link between the university and its local population.

7.9 An information and replica pack is being prepared for Standard Grade Latin classes by the Classical Archaeology Department of the Hunterian Museum, to meet the new Standard Grade requirement of 'investigation'. The Geology Curator at St Andrews creates displays for school visits which involve a three-hour exercise using a comprehensive questionnaire. Aberdeen's Natural History Museum receives some 50 visits each year from primary and secondary schools, the deaf school, mentally handicapped groups, local conservation groups and social clubs. The Talbot Rice Art Centre and Gallery is in regular contact with the Art Adviser for Lothian Regional Council, and runs structured visits where schoolchildren can work with exhibiting artists.

Further Education Programmes

7.10 Further education has not been neglected. Extra-mural and Open University classes occur in 20 cases, and there are diverse other initiatives in progress. The University of St Andrews, the SMC and the University of Glasgow are developing postgraduate courses in museum studies. Dundee's Anatomy Museum runs courses in respiratory anatomy for deep sea divers and biomedical engineers.

The Scottish Museums Council's Leisure Learning Programme

7.11 Several university museums have participated in the SMC's Leisure Learning Programme, which aims to attract new audiences to museums. At the Talbot Rice Art Centre and Gallery an artist, Janet Patterson, discussed her work with a 'Well Woman' group (none of whom had visited the gallery before), and visited the Occupational Therapy Unit of the Astley Ainsley Hospital—taking the gallery to the patients. The Collins Gallery at Strathclyde attracted children, over 60 per cent of whom were new visitors, to workshops based around an exhibition by the sculptor Dhruva Mistry. *Crystals in Industry*, an exhibition mounted by the Hunterian Museum and toured by the SMC, had a 'discovery day' for children and a dance workshop for all ages. As the Curator commented:

> Leisure learning activities extend the scope of the exhibition both in terms of furthering or deepening the participants' knowledge about some aspect of the exhibition and broadening the age and interest group attracted into the museum. This was particularly noticeable at the dance workshop which attracted those interested in modern and creative dance to an exhibition on *Crystals in Industry* which they would otherwise have been unlikely to visit (Stewart, 1988).

Activities such as leisure-learning programmes and outreach educational work have valuable repercussions in widening the student constituency and furthering contact with the local community. Scottish universities are positively recruiting students through schools liaison offices, and reaching potential undergraduates of all ages is necessary in an economic and political climate of response to market demand. However, work with schools, groups with special needs and community groups needs resources which can seldom be found where there is no salaried, professional curatorial presence within the university.

Modelling clay at the Collins Gallery, University of Strathclyde, in a Leisure Learning Programme workshop relating to the exhibition by the sculptor Dhruva Mistry.

Educational Use in Undergraduate Teaching

7.12 Despite changes in teaching methods, collections are essential tools in many subjects (pathology, anatomy, zoology, botany, archaeology, geology, music) and may become more so in others as research emphasis shifts. Anthropology has recently seen a revived interest in material culture, from the pre-eminence of social anthropology; the Curator of the St Andrews Ethnographic Collection plans to expand teaching of material culture, making the collection integral to a course, with changing displays and a designated project showcase giving students direct experience of objects. A course on material culture based on the Hunterian Museum's collections is designated a core course for Honours graduates in archaeology at Glasgow. Zoology collections have acquired new meanings and importance as ecology and conservation are brought into the syllabus.

7.13 Despite protestations that the role of universities is to educate, not to preserve museum collections, where material is integral to teaching it has an educational function as important as any other teaching device. Teaching collections need the protection afforded by a University Curator answering to a Collections Committee because while they may have little financial worth, they are valuable both internally and externally, though the latter is seldom recognized by departmental and university management.

7.6 Use of collections for enquiry services (incidents occurring)*

	Frequent	Occasional	Rare	Total	percentage of 69
Identification service	9	14	8	31	45%
General enquiries	9	15	6	30	43%
Research enquiries	13	20	9	42	60%

*30 collections were not used for enquiry services.

7.7 Limitations to development of enquiry services (incidents occurring)

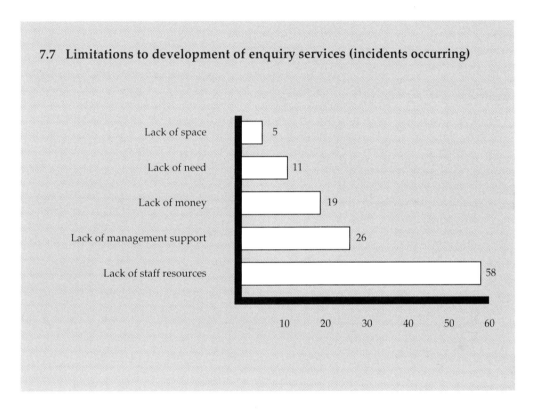

ENQUIRIES

7.14 Lack of staff resources makes extended enquiry services unlikely in all but the most fully curated collections, such as the Hunterian Museum and Art Gallery, which performs a national function in this regard. The Hunterian Art Gallery's Special Factor status is not reflected in financial recompense for its public role as the national enquiry centre for C. R. Mackintosh and J. M. Whistler. In 1986–87, 340 curatorial days were spent handling research enquiries from academics, students and schools, a substantial drain on staff resources. Half of these enquiries were from outside Great Britain. Provision of this internationally valued free service did not prevent the university cutting the Gallery's non-salary budget by 5.5 per cent in 1988–89. Within the Hunterian Museum itself, departments provide a significant national service by responding to enquiries at all levels ranging from identification of geological specimens to distributing information on Scottish archaeological sites.

7.15 Natural science collections offer some identification services, though at variable levels depending on staff resources. Medical science departments provide services related to identification

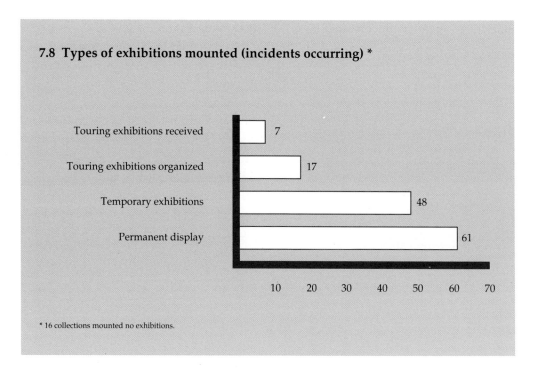

7.8 Types of exhibitions mounted (incidents occurring) *

Touring exhibitions received — 7
Touring exhibitions organized — 17
Temporary exhibitions — 48
Permanent display — 61

* 16 collections mounted no exhibitions.

through forensic science and pathology departments, but this rarely involves reference to collections. Responding to research enquiries may be part of the normal scholarly activity of a university department, for instance in the exchange of botanical specimens between herbaria. Informally, university departments frequently respond to enquiries of all sorts, but few would describe this as a collection-related activity.

7.16 The evidence that no development of enquiry services is likely or possible in 80 collections illustrates the effect of lack of management support and staff resources. Enquiry services beyond those specific to research could be regarded as part of a university's outreach work. Their development would need support from Public Relations Departments and university management. While universities may not wish to charge for scholarly enquiries, they could consider the desirability of charging for general enquiries.

EXHIBITION

7.17 Given that only nine employees in Scottish universities work full-time on

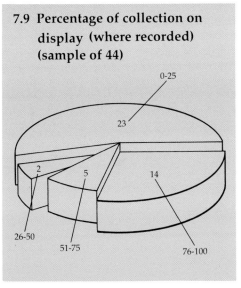

7.9 Percentage of collection on display (where recorded) (sample of 44)

0-25 — 23
76-100 — 14
51-75 — 5
26-50 — 2

collections, the fact that 61 collections have a permanent display, and that 48 mount temporary exhibitions is impressive, as is evidence that 17 collections organize touring exhibitions. Eighty-three of the 99 collections mount some sort of display, demonstrating that collections do maintain a comparatively high profile, and cannot be written off as hidden, and therefore disposable, assets. In 60 collections some development of the potential for exhibitions is seen as likely or possible.

7.18 Lack of staff resources is the prime

86

limitation to further development of exhibitions, cited in 53 instances. The vast majority of exhibitions are mounted by in-house staff, very occasionally with assistance from outside agencies. In a few cases outside agencies are entirely responsible. Despite access to the technical services generally on hand in large institutions, it is worrying to note that technical support is not available in 24 instances.

Co-operation with Other Organizations

7.19 Exhibitions are an avenue for co-operation between universities and other organizations. The Reid Collection of Historical Musical Instruments has recently mounted *Brass Roots: 150 years of brass bands* in partnership with Bradford Art Galleries and Museums. The Geology Department of the Hunterian Museum has a good track record of joint initiatives. In 1986 it produced an award-winning travelling exhibition, *Mr Wood's Fossils*, in association with Stan Wood, a private fossil collector and dealer. In 1988 its *Crystal Pavilion* in Glasgow's Garden Festival was seen by 1.2 million visitors. During 1989 the Geology Curator has been on secondment as a Director of Science Projects Scotland Ltd who plan to create a 'hands-on' science and technology centre based in Glasgow, the *Dome of Discovery*. This project is shared between two universities and four colleges who have contributed the core costs while money is also being raised through commercial sponsorship.

Quality of Displays

7.20 Quality, a judgement of design and content made by the project officer, is noted as high in 31 instances, (37 per

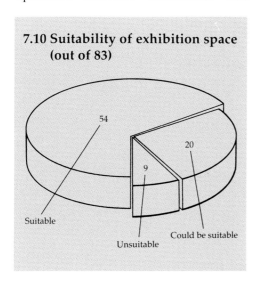

7.10 Suitability of exhibition space (out of 83)

54
20
9
Suitable
Could be suitable
Unsuitable

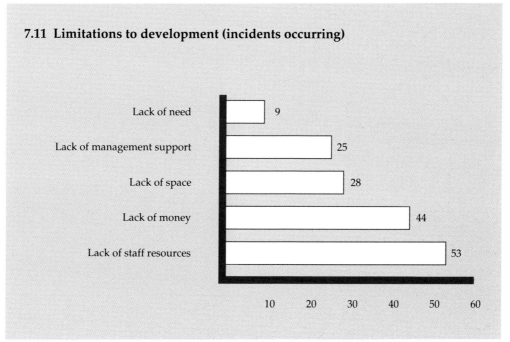

7.11 Limitations to development (incidents occurring)

Lack of need — 9
Lack of management support — 25
Lack of space — 28
Lack of money — 44
Lack of staff resources — 53

10   20   30   40   50   60

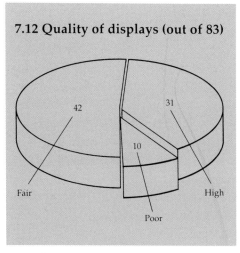

7.12 Quality of displays (out of 83)

42 — Fair
31 — High
10 — Poor

Museum won the title of Scottish Museum of the Year for its display on the history of the university, *An Overflowing Fountain*, and in 1984 and 1986 won Special Awards (Scottish Museum of the Year) for its new coin gallery and *Mr Wood's Fossils*. In 1987 university museums swept the board UK wide, with Aberdeen's Anthropological Museum being made Scottish Museum of the Year, and the Manchester Museum winning the UK award for its Egyptology and botany displays.

cent), and as fair in 42 instances (50 per cent). Curators have risen to the challenge of adverse conditions, the established university museums with full-time curatorial staff gaining a series of awards. In 1981 the Hunterian Art Gallery won the title Scottish Museum of the Year, in 1982 was named Art Gallery of the Year in the UK Museum of the Year competition, and has since won awards from the British Tourist Authority and the Saltire Society. In 1983 the Hunterian

7.21 Smaller scale successes are apparent, though unheralded, in departments throughout Scottish universities: in the foyers of the Physiology Department at Glasgow and the Dental Hospital at Dundee; in the Chemistry Department at Edinburgh and the Psychology Department at St Andrews. Archivists at Heriot-Watt, St Andrews, Edinburgh, Aberdeen and Dundee regularly mount temporary displays using both archives and artefacts. Dundee has used the opportunities afforded by large public spaces to turn parts of its focal Tower Building into exhibition areas. The ground floor foyer is enlivened by a display of photographs, the first floor has a new *Lamb Gallery* displaying paintings from the University collection, and a ground floor cloakroom has been converted into an area where students and teachers from Dundee Art School can display their work — exemplary use of previously 'dead' space.

An Overflowing Fountain. *The exhibition of the History of Glasgow University in the Hunterian Museum. A general view. Scottish Museum of the Year 1983.*

7.22 Recent initiatives include the Howietoun Museum of Aquaculture (Stirling); upgrading the Robertson Museum and Aquarium (Glasgow/ London); redisplay of the Pathology Museum in Glasgow's Royal Infirmary; redesign of the galleries of the Anthropological Museum and of the remaining permanent display areas of the Hunterian Museum; planned rehousing and redisplay of the Reid Collection, the Russell Collection, and the Patrick Geddes Centre (Edinburgh); planned touring and display of the Peto Collection at Dundee.

Exhibition Outreach Work

7.23 The Talbot Rice Art Centre and Gallery and the Collins Gallery generate their own temporary and touring exhibitions, and also act as venues for touring exhibitions from outside. The Scottish Arts Council supports both galleries with grants to the Talbot Rice for in-house and touring exhibition programmes, and 50 per cent funding for a full-time Exhibitions Organiser post at the Collins Gallery, indicating their importance in the overall spectrum of art gallery provision in Scotland. Several departmental and teaching collections circulate their own touring displays to libraries, schools and conferences, amongst them the School of Scottish Studies at Edinburgh, the Map Room of Aberdeen's Geography Department and the Civil Engineering Department at Strathclyde. Collections also lend items to outside exhibitions— the Talbot Rice's minor bronzes are on long-term loan to the National Gallery of Scotland, the maces from St Andrews and Glasgow were shown at an exhibition in Heidelberg and the Royal Museum of Scotland has borrowed items from some scientific instrument collections, while pictures and prints are commonly lent for exhibition elsewhere. Such loans entail some degree of risk so the University Curator and the Collections Committee should have the right to refuse to lend objects when it seems to them appropriate to do so.

Unexhibited Collections

7.24 Certain collections cannot be said to be exhibited at all; we have noted 16 examples. Herbaria are generally unsuit-able for display, as are human anatomical and pathological specimens where access is restricted by law (Anatomy Act, 1984). However, Glasgow's Botany Department mounted a display in Glasgow Art Gallery of the survey work done by its Community Programme, and Aberdeen's Anatomy Museum has contributed to exhibitions in Aberdeen Art Gallery. Lack of resources or inaccessible locations may also be reasons for non-display. The Classical Archaeology Cast Collection at Edinburgh is part of what the Curator of University Collections describes as the university's 'submerged museum'. Housed in a concrete shed in the Fine Art Department garden, it is sometimes seen by escorted students. Pieces date from the foundation of the Watson Gordon Chair of Fine Art in 1880, and the Department's early link to the Royal Scottish Academy's practical art teaching. Around 75 full-size casts of Greek, Roman and Romano-British sculpture have survived. Lack of curatorial time and money and limited access mean that the collection is physically deteriorating and losing its educational rationale. However, it is potentially both attractive and interesting, illustrating a significant era in the history of the University which could be exploited by proper exhibition, eg in a visitor centre.

OPENING

Factors Inhibiting Public Access

7.25 Public access to university collections is inhibited by both physical and psychological barriers. Inadequate signposting and parking, and lack of visitor services, are restrictions compounded by the less evident constraints of public reluctance to enter an exclusive world, where the bustle of university life puts an unfamiliar visitor in the unhappy position of outsider. The public are actually correct in their psychological

7.13 Limitations on development of opening collections (incidents occurring)

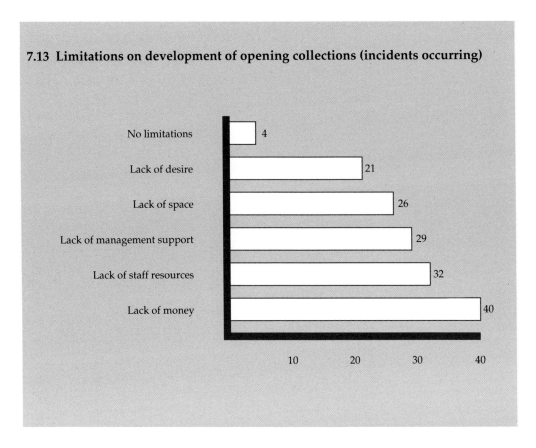

No limitations	4
Lack of desire	21
Lack of space	26
Lack of management support	29
Lack of staff resources	32
Lack of money	40

7.14 Prime factors inhibiting visits to university collections (incidents occurring)

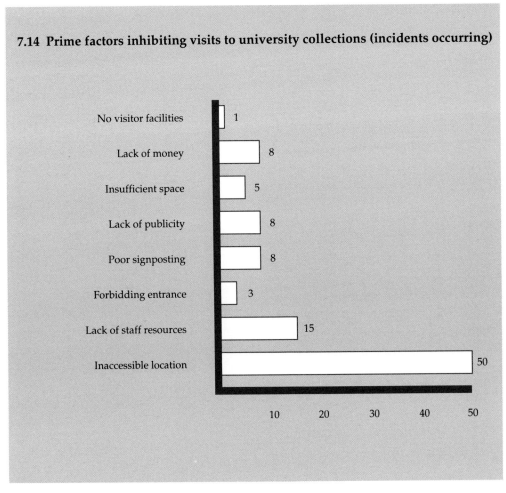

No visitor facilities	1
Lack of money	8
Insufficient space	5
Lack of publicity	8
Poor signposting	8
Forbidding entrance	3
Lack of staff resources	15
Inaccessible location	50

perception of what universities in fact are, that is private premises. The influence of these factors on visitor figures is manifest at Aberdeen's Anthropological Museum, where despite publicity for award-winning redevelopment, visitor figures are low at 18,000 in 1987–88. This compares with 440,860 in the same year for Aberdeen Art Gallery, only a short walk away. The Marischal College gateway entrance is forbidding, and signposts to the museum across the quadrangle are easily overlooked. The University will not allow visitor parking in the quadrangle, which has discouraged potential District Council funding for the museum. The galleries are on the first floor, with no lift access. The Talbot Rice Art Centre and Gallery occupies a comparable site (albeit in a city with a much higher international profile), with a first floor Gallery reached by crossing Playfair's imposing quadrangle. However, £60,000 spent on creating a ground floor entrance in 1987 immediately paid

off in visitor figures which leapt from 33,000 in 1986–87 to 41,153 in 1987–88.[7] It is to be hoped that redisplay of the Anthropological Museum's South Gallery, which includes provision for better signposting, will encourage visits to the museum. In 56 of the collections visited, in fact, the curators see potential for improving access.

Collections with Particular Access Restrictions

7.26 Access to collections of human anatomical specimens is legally restricted, while collections which are in constant teaching use, such as herbaria, and some geology and zoology collections, are only intermittently available to visitors. These are difficulties peculiar to teaching collections in universities and hospitals which need to be recognised by university and museum funding bodies. The MGC Registration scheme requires

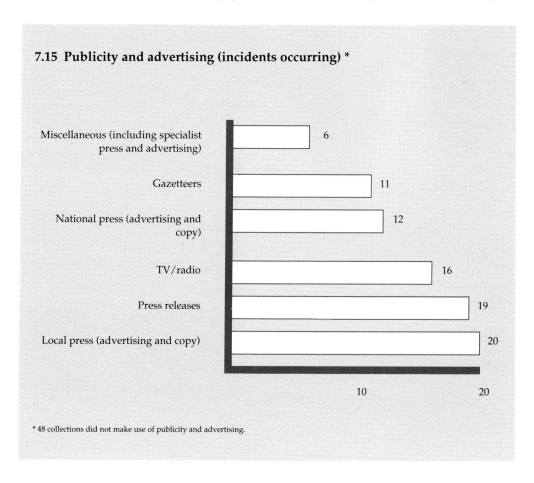

7.15 Publicity and advertising (incidents occurring) *

Miscellaneous (including specialist press and advertising)	6
Gazetteers	11
National press (advertising and copy)	12
TV/radio	16
Press releases	19
Local press (advertising and copy)	20

10   20

* 48 collections did not make use of publicity and advertising.

91

7.16 Internal activities and visitor services (incidents occurring) *

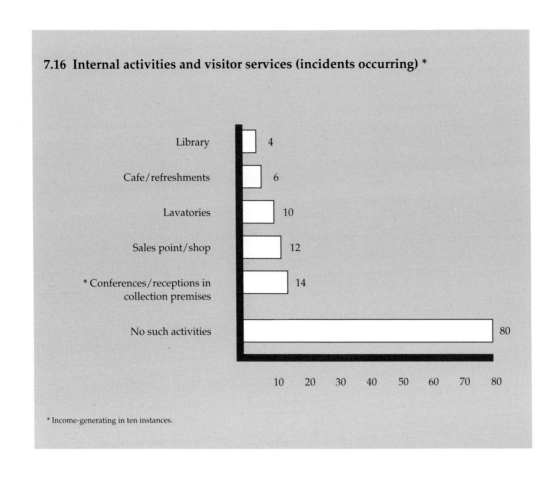

* Income-generating in ten instances.

7.17 Limitations to development of publicity and marketing (incidents occurring)

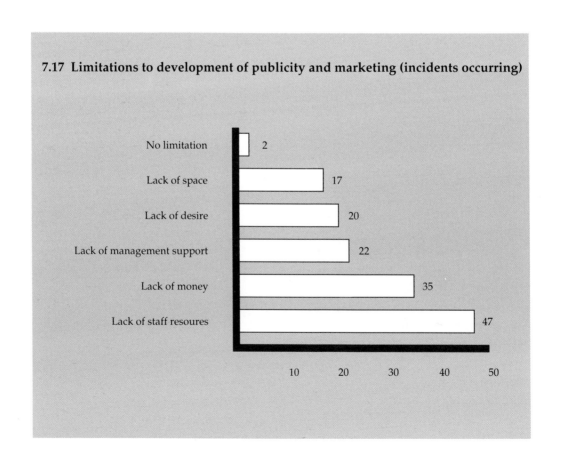

public access at some level, which must be specified and adhered to. The MGC accepts that there are restrictions on certain types of collections, and is willing to consider them for Registration if there is evidence of some public service provision. University Collections Committees should therefore be inclusive, so that inaccessible collections can be brought under their protective umbrella, especially if Registration can be applied to the university as a whole rather than to individual collections.

Overcoming Access Limitations

7.27 Overcoming barriers to public access needs help from Public Relations Departments, who have to tackle the fundamental difficulty of promoting collections that were accumulated in the process of education and research, not primarily for public edification. It seems curious that not one of the Scottish universities has a readily identifiable 'shop window', though the matter is being reviewed at Edinburgh, Heriot-Watt and St Andrews, and the Visitor Centre at Glasgow is being rebuilt in time for 1990.

PUBLICITY AND MARKETING

7.28 Forty-eight collections have no publicity mechanisms nor any publicity material, that is they produce no publications other than catalogues. Only 19 collections have the resources to run internal activities such as conferences, or to provide visitor services such as refreshments or sales points. In 56 cases it is thought unlikely that publicity and marketing will be improved, the major cited limitations being lack of money and lack of staff resources. None of the collections employs a public relations officer, though the Hunterian Museum and Art Gallery did so until 1988 under an MSC scheme. University collections have not

The removal of the statue of James Watt from the Chambers Street Building of Heriot-Watt University in July 1989.

allowed this shortage of resources to hamper their efforts to develop plural funding by marketing collections to sponsors, since we know that 13 collections are supported by earned income, and 23 by monies from fund-raising.

Marketing University Collections

7.29 The need to seek plural funding and to market collections has been well appreciated by university curators. The SMC's Policy Manual states:

> Professionalism in the marketing of museums must become commonplace, rather than a rarity, if they are to provide maximum value for money. Museums should be encouraged to improve their marketing either on a single or joint basis (SMC, 1988).

Universities are being encouraged to develop bullish marketing strategies. Heriot-Watt, the first university in Britain to have a Public Relations Department, has used its archive and artefact

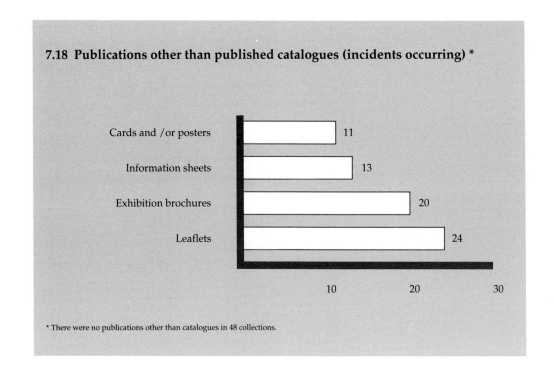

7.18 Publications other than published catalogues (incidents occurring) *

Cards and /or posters — 11
Information sheets — 13
Exhibition brochures — 20
Leaflets — 24

* There were no publications other than catalogues in 48 collections.

collection to significant advantage in campaigns which have attracted students and raised funding from commerce and industry. The office regularly issues press releases on matters such as the removal of a statue of James Watt from central Edinburgh to its campus site at Riccarton, or liaises with the Curator in compiling exhibitions. Some universities seem reluctant to highlight historical material because it is valuable but insecure, or because they fear to tarnish a progressive research image—not that this seems to have been a problem for Heriot-Watt.

Publications and Publicity Material

7.30 Prospectuses are a significant promotional mechanism for universities, and as we have observed, museums and collections are an important contact point between a university and the public, including potential students. However, it is disappointing to find that few prospectuses even mention their university collections. Strathclyde's undergraduate prospectus for entry 1989 goes so far as to use a colour photograph of the Burrell Collection to describe the cultural joys of Glasgow, ignoring the activities of its own Collins Gallery. By contrast, Aberdeen's prospectus gives a full account of four university museums, thanks to co-operation between the Information Officer and the Curator of the Anthropological Museum.

7.31 Voluntary or part-time curatorship is no bar to effective publicity and marketing. The Zoological Museum at Aberdeen, curated by a Senior Lecturer, and the Reid Collection of Historic Musical Instruments, run by an Honorary Curator, are examples of collections with a high public profile developed by regular contact with local and national media. The Hunterian Museum and Art Gallery took one year's advertising space in the Glasgow underground in 1988–89 (the year of the Garden Festival), believing that this would encourage visits from tourists, but found that it actually made little difference to visitor figures.

7.32 Through the focal office of a University Curator supported by a University Collections Committee university collections could develop co-operative publicity and marketing strategies which would diminish the current problems of scarce resources of money and staff time. As Public Relations Departments become more established in universities, and as university marketing becomes more sophisticated, collections should play a key role in helping to establish a university's corporate identity.

7.33 University collections can do much to help each other through organizations such as UMIS, and by contact with bodies such as the SMC, the Scottish Tourist Board and the Museums Association. The SMC has appointed a marketing manager with a remit to advise museums and collections on marketing strategies, and it is to be hoped that universities will make full use of this service.

SUMMARY

7.34 Given the shortage of resources, university collections are extensively used both internally and externally.

Their place in research and undergraduate teaching still exists, despite oft-repeated claims that collections are of diminishing academic value. Their role in encouraging public participation in educational activities, and in breaking down the barriers between universities and their local communities, is only now beginning to be acknowledged by university authorities.

7.35 Building on this achievement needs investment of time and money. Publicity and marketing schemes should be co-ordinated within universities by a University Curator and a Collections Committee, with support from the Public Relations Department. Visitor services need to be improved, with university visitor centres making full use of the material available in their own back yard. Universities now have the opportunity to capitalize on their cultural assets, and should not hesitate to seek help and advice from curators of local and national museums, and from outside bodies such as the SMC and the Scottish Tourist Board, to do so as effectively as possible.

8 SUMMARY AND RECOMMENDATIONS

INTRODUCTION

History of University Museums

The connection between universities and museums stretches back to the origins of both types of institution (1.1). The first public museum in Scotland was the Hunterian Museum at the University of Glasgow which opened in 1807, and collections transferred from the University of Edinburgh founded what became in 1904 the Royal Museum of Scotland (1.2–1.4). 19th Century enthusiasm for the educational value of collections saw museums being developed in tandem with teaching and research, and this pattern was revived by some of the new universities which opened in the 1960s (1.5). Despite episodes of disposal, usually relating to changes in research direction (1.6), university collections continue to accumulate objects which need resources of money, space and time to be properly curated (1.12).

Background to the Report

The state of university museums has been a cause of concern since the 1960s, with an escalating sense of crisis developing during the last 10 years of cutbacks in university funding (1.7–1.11). The Scottish University Collections Research Unit (SUCRU) was part of a concerted effort to address the matter by organizations of university curators such as University Museums in Scotland (UMIS) and the University Museums Group (UMG), in conjunction with the Museums and Galleries Commission and the Area Museum Councils (1.14–1.16).

Nature and Scope of this Survey

SUCRU was established in 1988 with the following broad objectives: to identify and describe collections held by Scottish universities; to recommend how their management, care and use might be improved; to identify sources of advice and financial support; to improve awareness of collections and provide a basis for decision-making both by individual Scottish universities and by the University Grants Committee (UGC)/Universities Funding Council (UFC). These objectives have been met by the Unit's fieldwork and by this report (1.17).

THE UNIVERSITIES AND THEIR COLLECTIONS

Types of Museums and Collections

Ninety-nine collections have been identified among Scotland's eight universities, 62 of which are held within individual departments (Table 2.1). Scientific instruments are the predominant type of material, though university support for collections tends to be concentrated on fine and decorative arts (2.5, Table 2.2).

Sources of Material, Size and Growth Rate

Passive accumulation is more common than active acquisition, purchase budgets being negligible even for internationally important collections (2.9, Table 2.4). The predominant sources for material are donation, bequest, fieldwork and, recently, transfer arising from UGC reviews (2.8–2.16, Table 2.3). As a result, collections lack the mechanism of directed purchase to control growth and orientation (2.14).

Importance of Collections

The importance of university collections

96

resides both in their function and in their intrinsic value (2.18). Material of little historic or artistic value may be vital to teaching or research, and more than half of the collections contain items which are categorised as professionally important (2.18). Intrinsic value is strongly represented by the 41 collections holding internationally important material (Table 2.4).

A list of Designated Collections should be compiled by a University Collections Committee. These should be recognised by the University Court and the UFC as having space and staffing needs which should be incorporated into management planning at departmental and university level.

Designated Collections should be those where the material is found by a Collections Committee to be significant in itself, to the history of the university, or to its current research and teaching activities. Collections not considered worthy of designation but which include individual items of interest should be assessed against disposal criteria adopted in a written collecting policy ratified by a Collections Committee. Professional advice should be sought in making such assessments.

MANAGEMENT OF COLLECTIONS

Collecting Policies

Written collecting policies which cover acquisition, disposal and ownership provide a baseline for good curatorial practice, and yet are in force for only ten collections (3.1, Table 3.1). The Scottish Museums Council (SMC) has asked its members (which include all the universities) to create management plans which should be in place when the process of Registration of museums in Scotland (1990–92) has been completed. Meeting this request will then be a criterion for grant-aid (3.2).

Ownership and Legal Title

Except where objects are privately owned or on loan, legal title to collections is held by the University Court (3.7), though there are areas of uncertainty where, for example, the local Health Board is involved (3.7, 3.8).

Disposal

Eighty-seven collections have no disposal policy, though 34 collections have suffered loss at some time (Table 3.2). Incidents of well-managed disposal do exist as models for other collections to emulate (3.15), but the risks of regrettable disposal are aggravated where there is no University Curator in post to oversee collections.

Written collecting and disposal policies should be laid down for all Designated Collections, and should be ratified by a Collections Committee and the University Court. Legal title must be recognized for all items within collections in order that each university knows the full extent of its rights and responsibilities.

Information provided in SUCRU collection reports should be used by universities to help create management plans for Designated Collections. Universities should consult the SMC regarding eligibility for Registration. Applications for Registration should be based on a Collections Committee's list of Designated Collections and should be co-ordinated by a University Curator.

Responsibility for Collections

Responsibility for collections is established in the majority of cases, whether formally defined or under an informal arrangement (3.18–3.21). However, without a University Curator and Collections Committee to sustain them, collections reliant on the work of an enthusiast (3.22), or where *de facto* responsibility is held by a member of the university staff (3.23), are vulnerable to the slightest change in funding, personnel, research direction or building use.

Clear lines of responsibility should be established between a University Curator and other Curators of collections in the university, and between a University Curator and a Collections Committee.

Organizational Contexts

Five of the eight Scottish Universities have active committees overseeing collections (3.24). Other organizational contexts for collections include key university offices, such as the Finance Department or Secretariat (3.26), the Estates and Buildings Department (3.27) and the Public Relations Department (3.28). Departmental autonomy (3.29) and links with external bodies such as those which exist between medical departments and hospitals (3.30), or between technical courses and industry (3.31), sometimes override connections with the corporate body of the university.

A Collections Committee should be set up within each university. To be effective, a Collections Committee needs Court and Senate representation as well as input from the Secretariat, the Estates and Buildings Department, and the Public Relations Department. The Committee should be served by an appropriately compensated University Curator.

MANAGEMENT OF PERSONNEL AND PREMISES

Curatorial Staff

The University Curator

Six universities now have a curator whose role involves overseeing university collections, though the extent of their actual influence varies widely (4.22).

Each university should appoint a University Curator, with adequate administrative support, able to oversee collections throughout the university. The University Curator should be responsible for all Designated Collections, and should be responsible to the Collections Committee. His or her title, responsibility and authority should be recognized throughout the university.

The University Curator should be an established member of the university staff. Where an existing member of staff has been designated University Curator, he or she should be allocated an appropriate amount of time to spend specifically on university collections and should be relieved of other duties without any loss of salary or status. The responsibility for managing collections, and research carried out on them, should be considered together in questions of promotion.

All matters relating to collections owned by the university should be referred to the University Curator. He or she should endeavour to raise curatorial standards for the university's Designated Collections, and to ensure that space, personnel or budgetary changes do not prove detrimental to collections.

Curators of Individual Collections

Only four museums employ full-time professional curators (Table 4.1), and only nine curators spend 100 per cent of their time working on their collection (Table 4.3). Curators may be employed as such, but have other duties (4.4), they may be in posts which have an acknowledged curatorial role (4.5), or they may have *de facto* responsibility for a collection because of their area of scholarship (4.6). Unfortunately pressures on university staff in the current climate of financial cutbacks constrain curatorial work, which may be perceived by management as peripheral to the main business of teaching or research (4.7).

The Academic Related scale is the most appropriate for curators of university collections because it limits possible warping of posts into teaching or research. It also places curators on an appropriate status and salary level, with promotion prospects beyond those for technical or clerical grades (4.9). However, only 26 curators are employed on this scale, compared to 61 curators in academic posts (Table 4.4). Ten curators have a museum background, while 76 are from an academic background (Table 4.2).

All Designated Collections should have a nominated Curator, accountable to the University Curator and the Collections Committee. This role should be recognised at departmental and university levels. Curators should be given resources to manage and document collections properly. Their responsibilities for managing collections, and research carried out on them, should be considered together in questions of promotion.

Where collections are large enough to warrant appointment of a full-time or part-time salaried Curator, the appointment should be made on an Academic Related scale. If they have a teaching commitment this should not exceed ten per cent of total curatorial time.

Support Staff and Other Staff

While vital to the proper running of collections, support staff are in short supply (4.11, Table 4.5). Carrying out technical, clerical and attendant tasks absorbs curatorial time, to the detriment of other aspects of the care and use of collections.

Other staff may be employed on government training schemes (4.14, 4.15), as contractors or consultants (4.17), or most often as volunteers (4.16). The change in government training schemes from Manpower Services Commission to Employment Training has hit this short-staffed area particularly hard, since the formal training component and the difficulty of selecting suitable trainees limit ET's value to university collections (4.14, 4.15).

Designated Collections should have enough access to support staff (technicians, attendants, clerical staff) to enable them to operate efficiently, and to ensure that collections are adequately protected from security and deterioration risks.

Training

Only sixteen curators have been able or willing to take up available training opportunities, a fact of some concern in view of the importance of the collections under their care (4.18). Access to training is restricted either by competition for funds (for academic scale staff) or by university prohibition on training and travel grants (4.18).

All curatorial and support staff, whatever their employment scale or status, should be eligible for training and travel grants from the university so that they can take courses in museum studies and preventative conservation such as those provided by the Scottish Museums Council, or the Museum Training Institute (4.19). Where university finance cannot be obtained, the Collections Committee should support such training from its own funds.

Premises

The majority of collections are adequately housed, though 28 are at risk from what are described as worsening circumstances (Table 4.9). Space compression and rationalization has meant that over the last five years, 27 collections have had to move, and 26 are either threatened with or have experienced recent loss of space (4.25, Table 4.7). Such disruption inevitably damages delicate objects and specimens, making insecurity of tenure a major source of anxiety to university curators (4.23). UFC space norms seldom allow for collections, which restricts universities in their effort to house them suitably (4.25).

Fifty-three collections share facilities on a permanent basis, permitting savings in overheads but exposing collections to physical risk from close proximity to material in regular use (4.24, Table 4.7).

Designated Collections should be housed in physically sound, secure premises. They should be considered in all space reallocation programmes, and should be duly provided for by the university when host departments are closed or transferred. The UFC should consider Designated Collections when applying space norms, and should meet the full cost of transfer or disposal arising from its recommendations.

University Courts should instruct buildings officers to allow display and storage space for Designated Collections during space reallocation programmes.

FINANCE FOR COLLECTIONS AND POLICY IN FUNDING BODIES

Sources of Funds

The foremost source of funding, available to 85 collections, is implicit support from the UFC's block grant as it filters through university space, services and staff costs (Table 5.1). However, the low level of explicit funding can be judged from the fact that 60 collections have no allocated budget, hampering efficient collections management and forward planning (Table 5.2). This is particularly disturbing when we consider that 41 collections hold items of international importance (Table 2.4).

The Universities Funding Council (5.2–5.10)

The UFC makes no direct contribution to financing collections, though it has denoted three in Scotland (the Hunterian Museum and Art Gallery in Glasgow, the Anthropological Museum in Aberdeen and the Russell Collection of Early Keyboard Instruments in Edinburgh) as Special Factors—activities which might be at risk because costs are above average, but which the UFC believes should be retained in the national interest (5.3). Special Factor funding is not earmarked, and information as to what it amounts to is difficult to extract (5.2, 5.3). However, it appears to have afforded some protection to the Hunterian Museum from financial cutbacks imposed at the University of Glasgow (5.4).

It is unclear what the UFC's attitude is to the policies of its predecessor body, the UGC, nor is it known whether the Special Factor will continue to be applied (5.5). Apparently the UFC will not carry out any further subject reviews (5.7). The UGC Earth Sciences Review has been implemented, and the UFC seem to have accepted their responsibility towards the transfer of collections resulting from the review's recommendations (5.8).

Designated Collections should be recognized as eligible for support from university funds. This funding should not be confined to implicit support; all Designated Collections should at least have

access to an identified annual budget, either channelled through the Committee or allocated by departments. Universities should ensure that collections are represented in budget estimates to the UFC.

Public Sources of Funds 5.11–5.17

Public bodies involved in funding university collections in Scotland include the Museums and Galleries Commission, government training agencies, the Scottish Education Department, the Scottish Development Department, the Scottish Tourist Board, the Scottish Development Agency and the Scottish Museums Council.

A specific structure leading from university collections to the funding bodies is needed. The UMG has been formally established to represent all university collections in the UK, including Scotland. It is recommended that direct and effective channels of communication should be established between the UMG and the UFC. University Museums in Scotland (UMIS) could offer advice to the Scottish Committee of the UFC on matters relating to university collections.

Designated Collections should be eligible for support from statutory bodies such as the Scottish Museums Council, the Museums and Galleries Commission, and other government agencies.

Local Authority Funding (5.18, 5.19, 5.20)

Local authorities barely contribute to the cost of running university collections, despite the schools services several collections provide (5.20). However, some co-operative initiatives are now developing which indicate the possibilities of further contact (5.19).

The Collections Committee should be empowered to raise funds which should be distributed equitably to benefit collections and services otherwise unlikely to attract support. Any monies accruing from the disposal of objects should be allocated for the benefit of Designated Collections.

Private Sector and Plural Funding (5.21–5.23)

Collections generate income from private sector sources (including charitable trusts) in 51 instances, and self-help through fund-raising and sponsorship is well developed, fund-raising being the second most commonly cited source of income (5.21, Table 5.1). However, it is difficult to raise money for the less public elements of collections care, or for collections which are not easily accessible, or where there is no salaried Curator with time to devote to fund-raising. Corporate fund-raising through Collections Committees might overcome this problem (5.22).

Plural funding is well established, with collections owned by the University of Glasgow tapping all twelve categories of funding (Table 5.1), and other universities with less sophisticated organizational structures still accessing the majority.

Sponsorship and fund-raising should be encouraged by the Collections Committee, which should identify opportunities within collections for raising money. All money raised should be retained for the benefit of Designated Collections without prejudicing any allocated university or public funding. Plural funding should continue to be developed.

The Collections Committee should be empowered to raise funds which should be distributed equitably to benefit collections and services otherwise unlikely to attract support. Any monies accruing from the disposal of objects should be allocated for the benefit of Designated Collections.

CARE OF COLLECTIONS

Conservation

Conservation was cited as a priority area for improvement in 31 collection reports, focusing on the need for professional assessment, for conservation plans, and for the application of preventative care and remedial treatment (Table 1.1). The predominant causes of deterioration relate to neglect and poor housekeeping, which could be alleviated in the short-term by training curators in preventative conservation, and in the long-term by instituting systems of curatorial control (6.2, Table 6.4). Sixty-five collections are not applying any preventative conservation measures, and only four have an emergency plan (6.4, Table 6.5). Access to professional remedial conservation and advice is hampered by shortage of money and by curators' unfamiliarity with available sources of grant-aid and treatment. The cost of conservation can be spread by co-operative ventures with other institutions requiring similar services, and such possibilities are being examined by several universities (6.9).

Although only four conservators are employed within the eight universities, technicians who can undertake skilled restoration mitigate the damaging effects of this lack of professional care. Scientific instrument and natural science collections are particularly at risk from cutbacks in technical posts (6.11).

Conservation standards need to be improved. All University Curators should have access to professional conservation advice, to training in preventative conservation, and to a realistic conservation budget.

Designated Collections should develop costed conservation plans for remedial and preventative treatment, in consultation with professional conservators and the University Curator. These plans should be ratified by the Collections Committee.

Storage

The impact of storage conditions on collections can be measured by the fact that 34 collections have 90 per cent or more of their material in store, 16 being entirely undisplayed (Table 6.9). Written collecting policies are a way of ensuring that growth rate does not exceed storage capacity (6.15), which has been cut by space rationalization programmes (6.14).

High density off-site storage repositories may be a sensible solution for universities where premises are becoming choked with seldom-used research material. Other options include sharing facilities with local museums, or subcontracting storage to an archiving company (6.16).

Secure, physically sound storage with long-term tenure must be provided for Designated Collections. The advantages of high density off-site storage should be considered by universities. It must be recognized that such facilities need curatorial supervision, for which adequate resources should be provided.

Documentation

Documentation is the most efficient mechanism for managing collections, yet lack of staff continuity and resources, particularly acute since cessation of MSC schemes in 1988 (4.14, 4.15), led documentation to be cited as a priority recommendation in 36 collection reports (Table 1.1). Self-devised systems are common, occurring in 45 instances, and are incompatible with those in other museums using standard Museum Documentation Association or National Museums of Scotland NAPIER systems (6.18, Table 6.13). Fourteen collections operate no documentation system at all, in many cases knowledge of the collections being held entirely by one person (6.19, Table 6.12).

Data gathered by SUCRU, which have been logged at the National Museums of Scotland, merely indicate the wealth and breadth of collections. Developing a full-scale documentation programme is a continuing priority for university collections. This could be run in association with the NMS NAPIER project which is intended to document museum collections throughout Scotland (6.20).

Documentation schemes within universities should be co-ordinated by University Curators, and should be compatible with NMS NAPIER or MDA systems. University Curators should maintain central registers of collections, to include up-to-date information on location and condition.

USE OF COLLECTIONS

Research

Research into university collections tends not to be recognized by the universities and the UFC (7.2). However, staff are using collections for research in 64 instances, and 44 collections are attracting outside researchers, to work on both systematic and historical material (Table 7.1). Lack of staff time to develop collections in specialised areas, to undertake research, to supervise students or to improve access by public-

ation, limits the benefits universities could accrue from research on collections (7.3).

Research by Curators on Designated Collections should be acknowledged to the same extent as other research and publication.

The research value of Designated Collections should be taken into account by the UFC. Such collections should be sufficiently funded that they can be professionally curated and developed to attract outside researchers.

Education

Despite changes in teaching methods, collections are still essential educational tools in many subjects, being used for undergraduate teaching in a total of 72 instances (7.12, Table 7.3). Though only the Hunterian Museum and Art Gallery at Glasgow employs a museum teacher, curators are managing to run guided tours, loan collections and special lecture programmes for visitors (7.6, 7.8). Work with schools, further education classes and participation in SMC Leisure Learning Programmes have valuable repercussions in widening the student constituency and furthering contact with local communities (7.8–7.11).

Collections which are integral to undergraduate teaching should be acknowledged as such by UFC funding and space assessment. The public relations aspect of outreach educational work should be recognized and developed by universities.

Regional Education Authorities should make a contribution, either financial or in kind (by seconding a teacher), to university collections which regularly run educational programmes for local schools.

Enquiries

Enquiry services could be regarded as part of the outreach work of universities, but attract a low level of management support and staff resources (7.16). Some collections are responding to national and international enquiries, and yet this public service is not acknowledged in their public funding (7.14).

Collections which provide a public enquiry service should receive acknowledgement for this in their public funding, and could perhaps make an economic charge for the service.

Exhibition

Eighty-three collections mount some sort of display, including permanent, temporary and touring exhibitions, demonstrating that collections do maintain a comparatively high profile and cannot be considered as hidden assets (Table 7.8). Prize-winning exhibitions have been mounted at the Anthropological Museum in Aberdeen and at the Hunterian Museum and Art Gallery in Glasgow, while smaller scale successes are apparent in numerous departments (7.20, 7.21). Co-operation with other organizations (7.19), creative use of space, and touring and temporary exhibition programmes all testify to the efforts of hard-pressed university curators, few of whom have access to technical back-up (7.18).

Certain collections, such as herbaria or human anatomical and pathological specimens, are unsuitable for public display though it might be possible to exhibit elements of these collections. Others are housed in inaccessible locations but could be represented in places such as visitor centres (7.24).

Display of Designated Collections should be encouraged by the Collections Committee. The university should support collections by making technical help for mounting exhibitions available to Curators.

Touring displays, or loans to collections outside the university, should be approved by the University Curator and the Collections Committee, who should have the right to refuse permission for objects to leave university premises.

Opening

Public access to university museums and collections is inhibited by physical and psychological barriers. Inadequate signposting and parking, insufficient information on access to collections, and lack of visitor services are restrictions compounded by public perception of universities as exclusive private premises (7.25, 7.26, Table 7.14). Public Relations Departments can play their part in overcoming such barriers, as can funding to enhance the physical environment (7.27).

Opening arrangements for Designated Collections should be assessed by the Collections Committee and, where necessary, improved by the university. Material from collections could be displayed when university visitor centres or 'shop windows' are created.

Designated Collections should have declared opening times and conditions, which can appear in gazetteers such as those published by the Scottish Museums Council, the Scottish Tourist Board and the Museums Association.

Publicity and Marketing

Although publicity devices such as advertising, publications (other than catalogues), and media contact are unused by almost half the collections (7.28, Table 7.15), the need to seek plural funding and to market collections has been well appreciated by curators, including those working part-time or voluntarily (7.29, 7.31).

Public Relations Offices, where they exist, have used collections effectively to heighten public and student awareness of university and departmental activities (7.29, 7.30), but more could be done to focus attention on collections both externally and internally by developing co-ordinated publicity and marketing strategies through the focal office of the University Curator (7.32). Universities are pursuing more sophisticated marketing strategies, and could use collec-tions to help establish their perceived identity.

Universities should recognize the potential value of their collections in promoting their own image and achievements. Designated Collections should be publicised and marketed more centrally, through Public Relations Departments, through visitor centres, and in promotional material, including prospectuses. Leaflets should be produced for Designated Collections, describing their contents and detailing access to them. Universities could seek advice on marketing and publicity from bodies such as the SMC and the Scottish Tourist Board and from curators of local and national museums.

BIBLIOGRAPHY

Arnold-Forster, K. (1989), *The Collections of the University of London*, London Museums Service, London.

Bass, H. (1984a), *A Survey of Museums and Collections Administered by the University of London*, presented to the London Museums Consultative Committee, unpub.

Bass, H. (1984b), *University Museums in South Eastern England*, Area Museums Service for South Eastern England, unpub.

Calder, J. (1984), *Royal Scottish Museum: The Early Years*, Royal Scottish Museum, Edinburgh.

Department of Education and Science (1973), *Provincial Museums and Galleries* (Wright Report), HMSO, London.

Department of Education and Science (1986), *University Forecasts*, Annex G, para 5.1, p 104, DES, unpub.

Fardon, R. (1988), *A Short Guide to the University of St Andrews' Ethnographic Collection*, University of St Andrews, St Andrews.

Goodhart, Sir Philip MP (1988), *The Nation's Treasures, a programme for our national museums and galleries*, Bow Publications Ltd., London.

Lord, B., Dexter Lord, G., and Nicks, J. (1989), *The Cost of Collecting*, HMSO, London.

Marshall, Alice J. (1970), *The Institute of Pathology, Glasgow Royal Infirmary, a perfunctory description of the building and itinerant staff covering half a century 1919–1970*, The Institute of Pathology, Glasgow.

Murray, D. (1904), *Museums: Their History and Their Use*, J. MacLehose & Sons, Glasgow.

Museums and Galleries Commission (1986), *Museums in Scotland*, (Miles Report), HMSO, London.

Museums and Galleries Commission (1987), *Report 1986–87*, MGC, London.

Museums Association (1986), *Museums Yearbook*, Museums Association, London.

Oxburgh (1987), *UGC Review of Earth Sciences*, UGC, London.

Ramer, B. (1989), *A Conservation Survey of Museum Collections in Scotland*, Scottish Museums Council/HMSO, Edinburgh.

Rolfe, W. D. Ian see Shelter, S. G.

Royal Scottish Museum (1954), *The Royal Scottish Museum 1854–1954*, Oliver & Boyd, Edinburgh.

Royal Scottish Museum (1984), *The Stewardship of the Royal Scottish Museum*, Royal Scottish Museum, Edinburgh.

Scottish Museums Council (1986a), *A Report on the Future Management of the Archaeological Museum of the University of St Andrews*, Scottish Museums Council, Edinburgh.

Scottish Museums Council (1986b), *Aberdeen University Museums*, Scottish Museums Council, Edinburgh.

Scottish Museums Council (1988), *A Framework for Scottish Museums*, Scottish Museums Council, Edinburgh.

Scottish Museums Council (1989), *Review of Local Authorities and Museums. Written evidence to the Museums and Galleries Commission's Working Party*, August 1989, unpub.

Scottish Tourist Board (1989), *Visitor Attractions Survey 1988*, Scottish Tourist Board, Edinburgh.

Shelter, S. G. (1969), 'The Herbarium: past, present and future'. In Cohen, D. M. and Cressey, R. F., 'Natural History Collections, past-present-future'. *Proc. Biol. Soc. Wash.* **82**, 559-762, Washington. Quoted in Rolfe, W. D. Ian (1979), Acquisition Policy in Palaeontology. *Special Papers in Palaeontology*, No. 22, pp 27–35.

Stace, H. E., Pettitt, C. W. A., and Waterston, C. D. (1987), *Natural Science Collections in Scotland (Botany, Geology and Zoology)*, National Museums of Scotland, Edinburgh.

Standing Commission on Museums and Galleries (1963), *Survey of Provincial Museums and Galleries*, (Rosse Report), HMSO, London.

Standing Commission on Museums and Galleries (1968), *Report on the Universities in relation to their own and other museums*, HMSO, London.

Standing Commission on Museums and Galleries (1970), *Eighth Report 1965–69*, HMSO, London.

Standing Commission on Museums and Galleries (1977), *Report on University Museums*, HMSO, London.

Standing Commission on Museums and Galleries (1978), *Framework for a System for Museums*, (Drew Report), HMSO, London.

Stewart, D. E. G. (1988), *Case Study 11: Hunterian Museum, Glasgow. Exhibition: Crystals in Industry*, Scottish Museums Council, Edinburgh.

Times Higher Education Supplement (Sept 1, 1989), *Times Higher Education Supplement*, No. 878, The Times Supplements Limited, London.

Warhurst, A. (1984), 'University Museums', *Manual of Curatorship*, ed. J. M. A. Thompson, Butterworths, London.

Warhurst, A. (1986), 'Triple Crisis in University Museums' *Museums Journal*, **86,** pp 137–140, Museums Association, London.

Willett, F. (1986), 'The Crisis in University Museums in Scotland', *Museums Journal*, **86,** pp 141–144, Museums Association, London.

Notes

[1] As recorded in a circular letter from the UFC to Vice Chancellors, April 1989.

[2] The Charity Commissioners' writ does not run north of the border. The Court of Session in Scotland is the body which provides variance of deeds of trust.

[3] The Anatomy Act 1984: 'An Act to make provision about the use of bodies of deceased persons, and parts of such bodies, for anatomical examination and about the possession and disposal of bodies of deceased persons, and parts of such bodies, authorised to be used for anatomical examination, and for connected purposes'.

[4] In a letter with note attached from the Chairman of the Committee of Vice-Chancellors and Principals to the Permanent Secretary of the DES, 21 July 1989.

[5] In a letter from the Minister for Education and Health at the Scottish Office of 24 February 1988, with an attached schedule containing the Secretary of State's responses to the individual recommendations of the Miles Report (MGC, 1986).

[6] A Survey of Collections (other than books and manuscripts) for Universities in the East Midlands. 73 departments were approached by the Project Officer, Nicola Rogers, and a summary of their responses was produced for limited circulation.

[7] These, and subsequent visitor figures quoted in this section, are taken from the *Scottish Tourist Board Visitor Attractions Survey 1988*, published by the STB.

LIST OF COLLECTIONS

Unless otherwise indicated the name of the department is the same as the name of the collection. Where collections are said to be open, this means that they may be visited by the general public during university or departmental opening hours. "Appointment" means that a visit may be arranged through the contact person. "SAO" means specialist access only; the collection is open to visitors with a special interest by appointment with the contact person, but not to the general public.

UNIVERSITY OF ABERDEEN, ABERDEEN AB9 1AS

Collection	Contact	Method
Anatomy	Dr M. Bruce	SAO
Anthropological Museum	Mr C. Hunt	Open
Forensic Pathology	Dr J. H. K. Grieve	SAO
Geography (Map Collection)	Mr L. McLean	Appointment
Geology	Dr N. Trewin	Appointment, some SAO
Herbarium	Dr C. C. Wilcock, Plant Science	Appointment
Natural Philosophy	Dr John Reid, Physics	SAO
Pathology	Dr G. B. Scott	SAO
Special Collections and Archives	Mr C. A. McLaren, Library	Appointment
Zoology	Dr R. Ralph	Open

UNIVERSITY OF DUNDEE, DUNDEE DD1 4HN

Collection	Contact	Method
Anatomy	Dr S. M. Bunt	SAO
Archaeology	Mr J. Robertson	Appointment
Chemistry	Dr John C. Barnes	Appointment
Art Collection; also Comparative Dental Anatomy	Dental School	Appointment
Geography	Mr W. G. Berry	Appointment
Geology	—	Closed
Electrical Engineering	—	Closed
Herbarium	Dr H. A. P. Ingram, Biological Sciences	Appointment
Historical Medical	Mrs L. W. Adam, Ninewells Hospital	Appointment
Manuscripts	Mrs H. J. Auld, Library	Appointment
Mechanical and Civil Engineering	Mr G. White, APEME	Appointment
Peto Collection (Photographs)	Mr Stanley Turner, Central Media Service	Appointment
Physics	Prof A. P. Cracknell, APEME	Appointment
Psychology	Dr Nicholas Wade	Appointment
University Art Collection	Mr R. Seaton, Secretary	Appointment
Zoology	Dr S. F. Hubbard, Biological Sciences	Appointment

UNIVERSITY OF EDINBURGH, EDINBURGH EH8 9YL

Anatomy	Prof M. F. Kaufman	SAO
Archaeology (Teaching)	Mrs Ann Morton	Appointment
Chemistry	Dr C. A. Beevers	Appointment
Classical Archaeology (including casts)	Dr R. L. N. Barber, Classics	Appointment
Forensic Pathology	—	Closed and disbanded
Geology (Cockburn Museum)	Mr Peder Aspen	Appointment
Herbarium	Dr P. M. Smith, Botany	Appointment
Historic Musical Instruments (Reid Collection)	Mr Arnold Myers, Reid Concert Hall	Open
Medical Archive[1]	Mr M. Barfoot	Appointment
Natural History	Dr P. Preston	Open
	Dr B. M. Matthews, Zoology	Wednesdays 2–4.30 pm or by appointment
Patrick Geddes Centre	Mrs S. Leonard, Outlook Tower, Castlehill, EH1 2LZ	Appointment
Pharmacology	Mr R. E. H. Deane	Appointment
Physics (Museum of Communication)[2]	Mr C. H. C. Matthews	Open
Russell Collection of Early Keyboard Instruments	Dr G. O'Brien, Music Department	Open
School of Scottish Studies	Dr M. A. Mackay	Appointment
Special Collections	Mr J. V. Howard, Library	SAO
Talbot Rice Gallery	Dr D. MacMillan	Open
University Collections	Dr D. MacMillan	Appointment

[1] This collection is owned by Lothian Health Board but housed in the university.

[2] This is a private collection partly housed in Physics and partly in Bo'ness.

UNIVERSITY OF GLASGOW, GLASGOW G12 8QQ

Hunterian Museum	Prof F Willett	Open
Including		
Prehistoric Archaeology and Anthropology	Dr E. W. MacKie	
Archaeology and Historical Collections	Dr L. J. F. Keppie	
Coins and Medals	Dr J. D. Bateson	
Mineralogy and Petrology	Dr G. P. Durant	
Palaeontology and Stratigraphy	Dr J. K. Ingham	
Hunterian Art Gallery	Mr C. J. Allan	Open
Anatomy	Prof R. J. Scothorne	SAO
Botany	Dr J. Dickson	Appointment
Chemistry	Mr I. C. McNeil	Appointment

Computing Science	Prof D. C. Gilles	Appointment
Geology	Dr A. W. Owen	Appointment
History of Dentistry and Comparative Dental Anatomy	Dr H. W. Noble, 378 Sauchiehall Street, Glasgow G2 3JZ	Appointment
History of Science	Dr P. Swinbank, Modern History	Appointment
Historical Ultrasound Collection	Mr J. E. E. Fleming, Queen Mother's Hospital, Glasgow G3 8SH	Appointment
Music (Hague Collection)	Dr W. A. Edwards	Appointment
Natural Philosophy	Prof R. G. N. Whitehead, Physics and Astronomy	Open, and Appointment
Marine Biological Station (Robertson Museum and Aquarium)	Dr P. G. Moore, Millport, Isle of Cumbrae	Open
Ophthalmology	Dr D. Holding	Appointment
Pathology	Professor H. Simpson	SAO
Physiology	Dr M. Gladden	Appointment
Statistics	Dr B. Torsney	Appointment
University Silver	Dr L. J. F. Keppie	SAO
Veterinary Anatomy	Dr S. E. Solomon	SAO
Zoology	Miss M. Reilly	Open

HERIOT–WATT UNIVERSITY, RICCARTON, EDINBURGH EH14 4AS

Archives	Dr M. M. Meikle, University Archive	Appointment
Pharmacology	Dr M. M. Meikle	SAO
Mechanical Engineering	Dr M. M. Meikle	Appointment
University Collections	Dr M. M. Meikle	Appointment

UNIVERSITY OF ST ANDREWS, COLLEGE GATE, NORTH STREET, ST ANDREWS, FIFE, KY16 9AL

Scottish Urban Archaeology Trust	Prof D. A. Bullough, St John's House	SAO
Maritime Archaeology	Dr Colin Martin, Dr R. G. W. Prescott	SAO
Anatomy and Pathology	Dr D. W. Sinclair, Biology and Pre-Clinical Medicine	SAO
Archives/Muniments	Mr R. N. Smart	Appointment
Chemistry	Dr D. Calvert (retd.)	SAO
Ethnography	Prof L. Holy, Geography	Appointment
Geology	Dr J. Kinnaird	Appointment
Physics	Dr E. M. Wray	Appointment
Psychology	Dr R. G. W. Prescott	SAO
University Collections	Prof M. J. Kemp, Art History	Appointment
Zoology (Bell Pettigrew Museum)	Prof P. J. B. Slater, Biology and Pre-Clinical Medicine	Appointment

UNIVERSITY OF STIRLING, STIRLING FK9 4LA

Institute of Aquaculture		SAO
(Howietoun Museum)	Mr P. Fairweather	
Airthrey Castle	Mr P. Fairweather	SAO
Archives/Library	Mr R. J. Davis	SAO
Biological Sciences	Dr D. S. McLusky	SAO
Press Room	Mr R. J. Davis	SAO
University Art Collection	Ms V. M. Walker	Appointment

UNIVERSITY OF STRATHCLYDE, GLASGOW G1 1XQ

Logie Baird Collection	Mr Adie, Manager,	Appointment
	Baird Hall	
Chemistry (Pure and Applied)	Dr R. H. Nuttall	Appointment
Collins Gallery	Ms L. Hamilton	Open
Surveying Instruments	Dr P. H. Milne,	Appointment
	Civil Engineering	
Mineral Resources Engineering	Prof G. Maxwell	Appointment
Pharmacognosy	Mr T. Moody,	Appointment
	Pharmaceutical Chemistry	
Physics	Dr T. Boag	Appointment